AF605136

How to Chase Change

Alexis Fernandez-Preiksa

How to Chase Change

30 Days to Master Your Mindset

SIMON &
SCHUSTER

New York · Amsterdam/Antwerp · London · Toronto · Sydney/Melbourne · New Delhi

HOW TO CHASE CHANGE: 30 DAYS TO MASTER YOUR MINDSET
First published in Australia in 2024 by
Simon & Schuster (Australia) Pty Limited
Level 4, 32 York St, Sydney NSW 2000
This hardback edition published in 2025

10 9 8 7 6 5 4 3 2

New York Amsterdam/Antwerp London Toronto Sydney/Melbourne New Delhi
Visit our website at www.simonandschuster.com.au

A catalogue record for this book is available from the National Library of Australia

ISBN: 9781761633485

Cover design: George Saad
Cover image: berkahlineart/Adobe Stock
Typeset by Midland Typesetters, Australia
Printed and bound in China

The paper this book is printed on is certified against the Forest Stewardship Council® Standards. RR Donnelley (Guangdong) Printing Solutions Company Limited holds chain of custody certification NC-COC-032126. FSC® promotes environmentally responsible, socially beneficial and economically viable management of the world's forests.

Contents

MODULE 4. DISCIPLINE

MODULE 5: THE NEXT CHAPTER

Introduction

I'm not one of those people who always knew exactly what I wanted to do with my life. While I'm grateful for my career in neuroscience, a field I absolutely love, it's not a career path that was always clear to me. For years, I actually had my sights set on being an actress, and for those that know me personally and have seen my extroverted personality in action, this makes a lot of sense. University, for me, was what I chose to do in the meantime while I waited for acting auditions and opportunities to roll around. I was twenty years old and had a lot of free time, and I wanted to sink my teeth into something apart from working at bars and nightclubs on the weekends, like the other aspiring actresses I knew. So I enrolled and selected a huge range of subjects, with psychology in the mix. It wasn't until halfway through the semester, when a guest lecturer gave a class on neuroanatomy, that I noticed I was hanging on to every word he said. I loved it. I wanted every class to be like that one, so at the end, I ran down the lecture hall to speak with him. He advised me to change my major to cognitive neuroscience, and I took his advice right away.

But after I graduated, neuroscience went on the backburner yet again, because I still held hopes of making it in acting. Another six years passed before I commenced my master's degree. In those six years between degrees (from ages twenty-four to twenty-nine), I moved several times: within the same city, twice to Paris, and then to Los Angeles. I had two big breakups, I quit acting, became super-involved in the fitness industry, and even thought I would open my own Pilates studio. Finally, I settled in Sydney, where at the age of twenty-nine I decided to study the brain again, an interest that stuck with me through all the chaos of my twenties. From day one of the course, I was hooked again.

My love for the brain has always been palpable, and even back then, I would try to find any excuse to weave fascinating facts about the brain into conversations. It was clear not only to me but to those who knew me that I had found my passion. Because I still had a love for performance – to this day, I'll take any opportunity to get on a stage! – I decided to combine performance and science and start my own podcast as a way to help me consolidate what I was learning by teaching it to others. I didn't know what to expect, but soon enough, the podcast started to spread through word of mouth, not only domestically but in all corners of the world. I found that people did not just want to be told what they should do to feel better, but they wanted to be told how and why, and to really understand the science behind what they were doing. I think now more than ever, people want to understand how their brain works on a deeper level so they can understand how to create change for themselves, and not just let life happen to them. And I love being able to provide that for as many people as I can.

Maybe you're at a turning point in your life, just like I was at twenty years old. Or maybe you're just looking to take a bit more time for introspection, to understand your thoughts and feelings on a deeper level than you have before.

Whatever it is you're seeking, I want to welcome you to *How to Chase Change*. My recommendation for you is to read this book one chapter a day, implementing the tasks and using the resources offered as you go. It's better to go slowly, and I would rather see you take more than the thirty days than rush through and brush over important exercises. Take your time, do the homework, and re-read modules that most resonate with you or the challenges you're facing at the moment. Later on, when you're in another stage of your journey or season of your life, I hope this book can be something you return to for support and guidance. Making time for yourself is always worthwhile, and reading this book is a perfect way to do just that.

P.S. I've also pulled together many great resources for you to explore outside of this book, which are all optional and a way of expanding on the concepts and knowledge from certain modules. Use these as much or as little as you like. While they are not necessary to get the maximum benefits of this program, they will allow you to dive deeper into the topics of interest for you.

MODULE 1

IDENTITY

Today is day one of thirty, the first step towards making changes in your life to master your mindset. During the next thirty modules, you will have access to tools that will help you procrastinate less, improve your focus, become more decisive and clear on what you want, feel confident in your own skin, feel more confident in your relationships, and feel happier and more satisfied overall. By putting into action certain behaviours, removing others, and simply changing how you approach your own thoughts, you will notice a difference in how you feel and how you show up in the world in a very short amount of time.

In this book, my aim is to have you focus on what you can achieve within your *own* mind. To do that, it's important to have a clear idea of where you are now and where you want to go, from a brain and mind perspective. This program is not about how to gain external or material things; it is focused on your internal power, and concerned with how you feel on a daily basis and your outlook on life.

Have you ever heard the saying, 'Fix your own home before you fix others'? Well, here I want you to work on your own home (your brain and mind) before you target all those other, external things. And that's why understanding identity is the most important place to start.

Now, before we get started, you may be wondering how the brain and mind differ. In this book, you will see me talk about the brain and mind as two intertwined but distinct things. While they are heavily involved with each other, and you cannot have one without the other, they are still separate. The brain is a physical organ, consisting of neurons, glial cells, blood vessels, fluids, and grey and white matter. It is separated into different regions that perform different tasks, and it can be observed. The mind cannot be observed directly: it is the intangible home of thoughts and all of our feelings and emotions.

Think of the brain as hardware, and the mind as software. Both influence each other significantly but serve a unique purpose. Exercises within the mind, regarding how you think and learn to process things, influence how regions of the brain may be connected and wired or strengthened. And changes in the brain, like injury, atrophy, or increases in volume caused by physical exercises, will impact your mind via your mood and your emotional and mental health.

The mind is the most variable factor when you look at happiness, performance, determination, and overall success.

It is what controls your physical self, what sets beliefs, what drives you or gets in your way; it is what determines if you will give up on something or keep trying. And understanding your mind begins with understanding your identity.

1.1 Get set up for success.

The first neuroscientific concept I want to share with you is something called a schema. This is, to put it simply, a way of thinking and behaving that you use to interpret and understand the world. It's how you organise the information that comes into your awareness for your brain to work more efficiently – and the brain loves efficiency! We have four kinds of schema: objects, self, roles, and events. And like a lot of processes in the brain, these can be edited and changed throughout your lifetime, several times over.

Jean Piaget, a Swiss psychologist in the 1900s, created a cognitive theory explaining how a person can change their schemas with the term 'adaptation'. According to his work, there are two different methods of adaptation: assimilation and accommodation.

Assimilation is where you incorporate new information into existing beliefs or structures. So, for example, if you were to come across a new piece of information that aligns with your current beliefs, then these things would integrate together and strengthen the current understanding or idea you have of the world. For example, imagine if you only ever saw black cats, and then one day see an orange cat. You would know by assimilation that this animal was also a cat.

Accommodation is different. This requires modifying and expanding existing cognitive structures. This may happen when we encounter information that challenges current ideas – something that forces you to actively adapt in order to accommodate these new experiences that do not easily fit in with your existing schemas. Let's say, for example, you were raised to fear or dislike a certain group of people. You believe, based on what you had been taught or how you had been raised, that these people are essentially bad. Then one day you have to interact with this group of people and realise they are fun, kind, and share similar values and beliefs to yours. This changes everything you thought you knew about them. So, you now have to dig into that belief pattern you held and restructure what you thought about this group. Because that belief was challenged, you can no longer go on believing what you did – it no longer makes sense in your mind.

This concept applies not only to the world around us but also as a kind of self-reflection. Accommodation is a great way of changing our beliefs about ourselves and what we are capable of doing, achieving, or having. If you can question your beliefs when necessary, you will be able to expand on your existing structures, challenging thoughts about your own abilities and what you deserve. That is exactly what I'm here to teach you: your ability to expand on your existing cognitive structures will show you a new way of experiencing your life, relationships, and the world. So be prepared to do a lot of accommodating in the next thirty days. Especially when it comes to statements about yourself.

The next concept I want to explain is cognitive bias. This is when people create their own version of reality based on how they perceive information that is coming in, and not necessarily paying attention to all the objective information that's in front of them. An example would be saying something like, 'Everyone in this city is rude,' then constantly highlighting all the rude encounters you experience. You're not paying attention to the people who are polite, and you use the evidence of the rude people to confirm your belief, ignoring all other information in front of you. Or, you could say, 'All men are arseholes,' because you had a bad experience with dating a few men, and have seen some of your friends in bad relationships with men. This becomes your bias, and it's difficult for you to give a great man a chance, or to admit how great other men are because you're always looking for instances and examples that confirm this bias. Anything that negates this bias is overlooked.

Cognitive bias does not align with logic or reasoning, but it does shape how we make decisions, how we behave, and how we judge things outside of ourselves. In the modules to come, I will give you many examples of how you may be biased to believe something, and how you can challenge those beliefs to change how you experience the world. As you become more self-aware, you will start to notice many areas in your thought processes where you hold a bias, and where that bias can be detrimental for you. Learning to debate with yourself and argue both sides is a great way to challenge any bias you may hold, which will help you not only become more open-minded but also process pain and adversity in a healthier way.

As you are starting to see, you hold an incredible amount of power in your own mind. And right now, we want to channel that power towards goal setting. I want you to understand the importance of having a goal that is tied only to the progress you make within your mind. I want you to see what that would look like, and how that can be measured. Because when you understand what it feels like, you can seek it out.

Having goals that involve things outside of you (relationships with others, careers, many experiences, family) are awesome. But without nailing the goal of strengthening the mind first, it's a game of luck. Will I have a healthy relationship? Will I have a career in which I succeed and thrive? Can I get all the money I dream of having so I can pay for the things I want? *So* many of these answers can be unlocked by first addressing your mindset.

Your daily task

I want you to get clear on your existing schemas. These are your current beliefs around what you think you are capable of having, feeling, achieving, and receiving based on who you are today. These are different from goals and aspirations. For example, you may wish to be someone who could run a marathon, or to set yourself really difficult tasks and see them through, but, as of today, you do not actually think you could accomplish this. Notice the difference between a dream for your ideal life versus an understanding of what you currently believe you are capable of.

Your schemas can be edited and changed throughout your life, but as a starting point, I want you to get super clear on what that looks like. This way, you know which areas you would like to investigate and work on throughout the next thirty days.

First, write down categories (you choose how many you want). For example, categories might include:

- Career
- Relationships
- Health (mental and physical)
- Abilities (these can be hobbies but can also be skills outside of your career)
- The outside world (this is all the beliefs you hold about the world around you: Are you optimistic, pessimistic; do you feel there are opportunities everywhere you look; do you think you are doomed and everyone is out to get you?)

And then, under each category, just list your feelings and beliefs on that subject. For example, under career you could write:

- I'm struggling to find my passion.
- I am good at working hard for others.
- I do not believe I am good enough for a promotion or dream job.

They do not have to be negative, though; they could also be things like:

- I am the best person for this job.
- I love challenges, because I always overcome them, and that's why people can rely on me.

Take the time to do this for each category. Just the simple task of writing down these beliefs and getting acquainted with where you are will make it easier for you to make the most of all the other tasks in this program. Brainstorm it all and don't hold back. This will be a great exercise in self-awareness, and in understanding what your schemas are.

You cannot change what you do not acknowledge, so today, I want to make sure you are really aware of where your mindset stands. When it comes time to crack it all open and do a mental spring-cleaning, it is all there for you in plain sight, and not hidden away like something you are afraid of.

1.2 What is your purpose? Do you really need one?

Purpose can be intimidating. The narratives we have all heard about finding your purpose make it feel like it needs to be something you come across and instantly recognise as your one and only calling.

A purpose is simply a meaningful and motivating aim of your life. It is your reason for being here, and it helps you form your goals and keep you on track. It creates meaning in your life, and it feels satisfying. For some, this is linked to their work and career, but for many, it is something separate. That said, I do believe that purpose does have to be linked to making yourself useful; not turning yourself into a martyr and living purely for others but contributing in some way. Connection and community are such an integral part of the human experience, and knowing you are a part of your community and you provide value is important in feeling like you have a purpose.

There is a lot of pressure on the concept of purpose, because we hear about people that may have done huge generous acts or started charities or influenced millions of people. You may see someone living out a career of helping save lives, such as a doctor or neurosurgeon, or you hear about people reaching millions with their music or art, and while these stories are a true representation of finding purpose, they can make others feel that purpose has to be this larger-than-life thing, making it seem unattainable. But I think this can be misleading; it is sometimes the most simple things in life that keep people feeling like they have a reason for being here on this earth. And by simple, I don't mean trivial or unimportant. Many people that make it past one hundred years old claim that they maintain their health because they always do something to contribute, and that is their purpose. So maybe, if you are not yet clear on purpose, it's time to rethink what it could look like.

So let's start with some questions to ask yourself:

- Do you think that purpose is found by searching, or do you think that purpose finds you?
- How have you defined purpose in your life previously? If you were to name three people you know who are definitely living their purpose, who would they be, and what is that purpose they are living?

Take a moment to think through these questions. Understanding how you look at purpose will help you understand why you may have struggled to feel it in the past.

Now, let's go back to that first question: I think, for most important things in life, you have to go after them, and not wait for them to land in your lap. This goes for passions, relationships, jobs, personal style, lifestyle, and of course, purpose. If you believe that purpose finds you, and you need to just be patient until it arrives at your front door, then consider this question: Does the level of activity and interaction you have with the world increase the chances that your purpose will find you?

In most cases, I do not believe that purpose slaps you in the face. It is normally triggered by a few events that lead you to have an aha moment of 'I've found it!' But if you feel like your day-to-day life is on repeat – same job, same place, same people – and you are searching for something more, then *how* is purpose ever going to find you? *You* need to find *it*. And it is found though identifying a certain feeling, and then going after that feeling.

Have you ever done something for someone and not even wanted recognition for it, because the feeling of having done it is so great on its own? Or have you ever put your mind towards a task or contributed to a project, and then felt elated and couldn't stop thinking about it? Maybe you were left wondering how you could contribute more or become more involved? Have you ever been able to talk someone out of a bad state and get them feeling light and happy again, and felt great that you could offer help? Have you ever brought a dying plant back to life and felt superhuman for doing so? (Okay, this is very specific, but I definitely have, and it is underrated.) These feelings can all be connected to purpose, and help you identify yours.

What is purpose, really? Your purpose is your 'why'. It's that feeling of contentment within yourself, the feeling of being exactly where you need to be. Do you need one? Yes, I believe everyone needs a why. But I don't believe it has to be limited to one thing, or that it has to be something huge.

I've also found that purpose is an excellent compass for your mood. When you are feeling depleted, flat, sad, or disconnected, you simply have to look at how in touch you are with your purpose.

Personally, I found that purpose helped me get through my second heartbreak surprisingly fast in comparison to my first heartbreak. In my first, I was twenty-six years old, and I spent so much time with my head in the past, hoping for things to return to the way they were. I felt super out of touch with anything that made me happy, which then made me feel even more isolated. I would try to numb my own feelings by being on social media, and I felt distracted or just plain sad a lot of the time. It really took me a long time to work my way out of that, as I did not have a compass to pull me in a direction of feeling fulfilled.

At the time, I did not have a strong sense of purpose, but, being young and in love, it was not something that I noticed. Often, as you mature, you start to understand the need for more meaning in your life, while your twenties are more a time for learning and exploring, which is equally important. I learned through this experience that my relationship was not my purpose, and the breakup made me realise I had been placing a lot of my happiness in the hands of someone else.

Fast forward to my second heartbreak, which was arguably worse than my first; loads more drama that made for juicy stories months after the breakup. But strangely, I recovered so much faster. Not only because I had experienced heartbreak before, so I knew what to expect, but because I had a *why*, something that was pulling me out of bed every morning that I needed to work on, a long-term goal that mattered to me more than my short-term sadness. I had something I could throw myself into and dedicate myself to: the pursuit of my neuroscience degree. I had decided, in the depths of my sadness, to enroll in my master's program and finally succumb to my years of wondering what it would be like if I dedicated my time to studying the brain (again).

This was a pivotal point in my life for many reasons, but most importantly, it was the first time I felt a deep connection to a purpose. Even through my saddest post-breakup moments, it felt important enough to keep pushing. And I found the more I threw myself into this subject that I loved so much, the better I felt and the less I fixated on my heartbreak or feelings of rejection. I even started to love myself and respect myself more – and after the relationship I had just come out of, my self-love and self-esteem had taken a major blow and needed some rebuilding.

For the first time ever, I knew clearly what I wanted. I did not know the exact direction my career would take me; I actually had no idea where I'd end up. But I knew that I wanted to pursue neuroscience in some way, and there was no question about it. Before I knew it, I was completely healed from the heartbreak, because every time I was sad, I had this emotional compass, this pull to do something that just felt right. And after following the feeling of my 'why', more and more opportunities started unfolding for me. This eventually got me to my career of creating the podcast, writing, teaching people what I had learned and being able to connect with and help others. And who knows where it will continue to take me? It is not about knowing the end goal, it's about identifying the feeling that you get when you dedicate your time to something that feels just right for you.

You will notice your self-love improving the more you work on this feeling and this 'why'. If you are someone who is supercritical of your appearance and compares yourself with others all the time, then this will be an absolute game changer for you. It will take you from thinking that your appearance is a major factor in what you have to offer the world to realising that your value as a person comes from how you connect with others and how you fulfil that sense of purpose. When you tap into that, you will start to truly love yourself the way you are. It gets you out of your head and out into the world feeling connected.

But don't just take my word for it: a lot of research has been done on the benefits of having a purpose, and how that impacts people's overall levels of happiness and their ability to regulate their emotions. A study published in PLOS ONE in 2013[1] found that having a purpose in life can improve your emotional recovery after negative events and increase resilience by increasing automatic emotional regulation. It went so far as to say that purpose in life is a great predictor of health and longevity. When people have a purpose, they are more likely to reframe how they view stressful and painful situations to recover faster and deal with these things more productively, just like I did with my breakup. It did not remove all my sadness, but it set me on course for a steady climb upward until I felt healed again.

And if you can link your purpose to spending time helping others, then it comes with even more mental-health benefits. A study published in 2023 from Ohio State University[2] found that when people performed acts of kindness, they led to improvements in symptoms of depression and anxiety, and helped improve people's connection with others. These results demonstrate that connection with others is key to improving your overall happiness, and works as well as other interventions to treat symptoms of depression and anxiety.

But it is important to note that when it comes to identifying purpose, it has to feel good to *you*. Doing something that you dislike just because you think it will make you a better person may be kind and charitable, but that doesn't make it your purpose. When you find it, you will feel it, and you will know it. It feels the way you feel when you smile at a stranger and they smile back. Simple, and fulfilling.

Before we close out this module, allow me to make something clear: purpose should be linked to feeling useful, and that is done by contributing to something outside of yourself. Be it your community, your environment, or whatever it may be, you are contributing. However, it still must also serve you at the same time. A purpose is something that fulfils you as an individual, that serves you but also makes you feel useful. It is not living your life for someone else, like your partner or your children. It should never be about suffering for the good of someone else; that is not a purpose. As you try to determine what it may be, you will do what makes you feel useful and fulfilled, while also filling up your cup. That is the feeling you're chasing.

Your daily task

If you are struggling to find your purpose or understand what that looks like, try zooming out and focusing on a feeling instead. Write a list of moments when you feel fulfilled and connected (to others, to nature, etc.). Even if it is just a fleeting moment.

For example:

I feel connected when...

- I help a stranger pick things up off the floor
- I compliment someone
- I make someone laugh or entertain someone
- I teach someone to do something new
- I water my plants/garden
- I spend ten minutes playing with my dog
- I inspire or encourage someone

Now think about what you could be doing day-to-day to get more of these feelings. A lot has to do with interacting with the outside world and feeling good about your actions and interactions. It is difficult to feel a sense of purpose when you are feeling isolated and disconnected. Once you figure out what feels best, set the goal of doing one or more of these things on your list – the things that make you feel connected and good within yourself – every day this week. That feeling is you connecting with your purpose, and the more you lean into these things, the more opportunities present themselves for you to have more of the same. They start small, and before you know it, you will be discovering interests and passions that you didn't know existed.

1.3 Learn self-awareness – the key to unlocking your progress.

Our last chapter was all about the wonderful feeling of finding your purpose. But in order to really transform our mindsets, we've got to confront our negative emotions as well. How well can you critique yourself? Are you any good at it? Or do you avoid it at all costs? You may look at critiquing yourself as negative self-talk, but there are important differences between the two. Let's distinguish them clearly before we move on.

Negative self-talk is when you put yourself down, often with no way of resolving a concern, or no optimistic outlook as to how you will move forward. It is basically character assassination, making general statements about who you are as a person, such as: 'I am a failure', 'I am not smart', 'I can't make friends', 'no one can love me', 'I always give up', 'I never win.' And these statements only serve to make you feel smaller. They lead you to retreat or pull away from a challenging moment. You never feel empowered or better about a situation after engaging in negative self-talk.

Critiquing yourself is different. Here, you are looking at the good and the bad, assessing your behaviour, looking at what is working for you and what is not, and coming up with a plan. How can you change things about your behaviour that are within your control? How can a challenge work for you instead of against you? You don't make generalised comments about your character, you are clear and specific, simply looking at behaviours or actions with an objective lens.

So, the next time you make a mistake or have an argument or hurt someone, don't let emotions overwhelm or get the best of you. Pay attention to how you think about yourself or speak to yourself in that moment, and ask, 'Is this negative self-talk, or is this self-awareness that will help me do better next time?'

This concept is something we will touch on again in later chapters, but your relationship with yourself is the most important one you have. And any good relationship is built on good communication. You need to get good at talking to yourself in a way that will help you grow. Changing how you critique yourself will have a positive impact on your relationship with yourself, as you will be better at identifying what needs to be changed. When you're awful to yourself, instead of getting to the bottom of the issue, you leave yourself likely to reach for things to pacify how you feel and distract yourself from pain. You avoid addressing the reality of the conflict, and this then makes it harder to be self-aware in the future. When the dust settles, you may shift the blame to other people or situations rather than learning a valuable lesson.

Here is an example of someone who had always avoided critiquing his own behaviours, who was never willing to own up to mistakes, and what changed for him the moment he became self-aware.

A listener wrote in to me recently, telling me how his marriage had been going downhill for a very long time. He explained how he felt that his wife was pulling away from him, and she was hiding things from her past. She would avoid talking about her past whenever he would try to bring it up, reinforcing his belief that she had something to hide, which made him feel even more insecure within the relationship. He would then get upset with her, and this would cause huge arguments. They had been married for more than fifteen years and could not escape this pattern.

He then listened to one of my podcast episodes on retroactive jealousy. Retroactive jealousy is where you feel threatened by your partner's past, normally your partner's past relationships. This causes you to engage in what are called seeking behaviours, like going through your partner's old photos on social media or going through their ex's social pages looking for information, which causes constant comparison, seeking validation from your partner that you are good enough or 'better' than their past relationships. It can cause you to make mean or sarcastic comments, and it drives a divide between you and your partner, as there is nothing they can do to change the past and make you feel better.

And for the first time in his marriage, this listener realised that there was an issue in *his* behaviour. He had been jealous of his wife's previous partners, trying to get her to constantly reassure him about his insecurities, while also making her feel guilty that she'd had relationships before him. The things he was fixated on were all in the past and completely out of his control. Plus, the things upsetting him were things that she was completely within her rights to have: past relationships and experiences.

In his letter to me, he said that he had an instant moment of realisation. An aha moment. Finally, what she had been telling him all these years made sense: she was only avoiding talking about her past because he had demonstrated time and time again that he would react negatively to whatever she said. She did not have anything to hide; she was just sick of his outsized and unfair reactions. He was finally able to see his behaviour for what it was instead of avoiding it. And by noticing it, he could try to fix his marriage by breaking this pattern. He asked his wife to listen to the episode with him, telling her that he believed he was displaying retroactive jealousy, and he wanted to address it. This action let her know that he finally understood her. After listening, his wife felt heard for the first time, and was so happy that he was able to see how his behaviour was hurting her. They were able to have a truly open and honest conversation. He told me his marriage had been saved. Had he not admitted to his behaviours and realised the impact of what he was doing, he not only would have ruined the marriage, but he could have entered into every other relationship behaving the same way.

So many issues in our own relationships come from an inability to see the wrong we have done or to see our behaviours from someone else's point of view. And so often we will attempt something we have failed at in the past without looking at what we did wrong and trying to address it before going again. Awareness is the key to being able to edit and improve yourself in all aspects of your life.

Now, I realise that being told something is wrong with your behaviour is unpleasant, to say the least. Our instinct is to defend our position, to dig in and prove ourselves right. But why do we get so defensive? What is defensiveness, anyway? It is both a feeling and behaviour that stems from someone being critical of you, which normally leads to feelings of shame, anger and sadness. It is actually a protective mechanism, to distract or shift focus so that you can temporarily feel better after being 'attacked'. But while this works to protect us in the short term, it actually makes things worse in the long term, because you never learn to accept criticism and deal with it in the moment. Accepting the criticism *will* make you exposed. And that defensive impulse is telling you that if you admit you are wrong in this one instance, then you lose credibility, and this person you disagreed with will now believe that you are wrong in everything else. And if this happens, it will mean they will have the upper hand and you will have 'lost'.

But relationships are not a contact sport, and there is no scoreboard. Being vulnerable is never as bad as you predict it will be. There is always a silver lining to being vulnerable. Let me be clear: the fear of vulnerability is very real! But the more you avoid it, the scarier it becomes. Not only are you suffering internally, avoiding change, avoiding growth, but you may also be harming your relationships unintentionally, because it is so difficult to admit to being wrong.

But understanding your shortcomings and admitting when you mess up will more likely have the opposite effect on those you love. Like the example I gave earlier in this chapter, this man's wife respected him *more* when he opened up to her and highlighted his own misguided behaviour. He said, 'I hear what you are saying, I see what I have done, and I want to make improvements.' This is far from a weakness. Willingness to be exposed is true strength, a powerful choice from which everybody benefits. Not to mention how attractive it is when someone does that for you. It oozes self-confidence and self-awareness. Who doesn't like being told they're right?

Your own intuition will do some of the work here – sometimes you just *know* you're wrong, no matter how hard it is to admit to yourself. But you will also gain so much from seeking out and being truly open to outside opinions. Sometimes you could be told something a thousand times by your partner or family, but it takes hearing it from someone else – a stranger, therapist, or a book explaining it in a different way – to resonate, just like that podcast listener I told you about. Suddenly the penny drops, and you finally see what others had been saying all along. The more work you do on looking into yourself and your behaviours, the more aha moments you have, and the easier it is to realise what's really going on.

What will you gain when you start to become self-aware and able to critique your behaviours? Power. But not the superficial kind of power, where you control or try to control others through intimidation or manipulation. The deeper, internal kind of power that shows how comfortable you are with yourself, and how open and willing you are to hear suggestions and take them into consideration. Only those who are truly comfortable in their own skin are not afraid to admit that they could do better or do something differently. They know that one mistake does not determine or change who they are as a person.

Additional resources

If you want to access more tools to become self-aware and unlock your progress, I recommend the book *Atomic Habits*, by James Clear. Another great resource to become aware of how your mind operates and how thoughts take over is *The Power of Now*, by Eckhart Tolle.

I also have a podcast episode that dives into self-awareness and how to use it to create change. It is episode 252: Self Awareness: You can't change what you won't acknowledge.

1.4 Change how you look at your capabilities.

Do you believe that it's luck that got you where you are? Skill? Raw talent? Or consistent, hard work? How about those around you? How did they achieve their greatest accomplishments? Was it all within their control? Or was it due to external circumstances, such as birthright or natural, born talent?

If you tend to look at successful people and believe that external factors are the reason they got to where they are, then you may always feel restricted in what *you* can do with your time. This is a perfect example of cognitive bias, which we discussed earlier – as a reminder, cognitive bias is the phenomenon where people create their own version of reality based on how they *perceive* information, without necessarily paying attention to all the objective information that's in front of them. If you believe that people who do well are born into money or privilege or a great network, you may never want to change your mind. Even if I present to you one, two, ten examples of people who pushed past what they originally thought they were capable of, whether that's income, learning capacity, physical achievement, mental-health journey, etc., then you may label those examples as 'outliers'. You may think it won't ever be like that for you. How many examples would you need to be convinced that you have a huge influence in determining the limit to your abilities?

Granted, there are certain things that will restrict you from achieving certain very specific goals, like height or weight for a sport, or certain physical traits needed to do some tasks or jobs. But more likely than not, you're selling yourself short. How much credit do you give your brain and its ability to learn skills and retain information? What about your physical body and its ability to become stronger or heal? Have you put a ceiling on what you think your body and mind can achieve?

Personally, I never loved studying when I was in high school. I wanted to be an actor, as you know, so I couldn't be bothered with science or mathematics. I chose subjects such as dance, drama, and art, and I never wanted to go to university. So much so that I didn't even bother applying after high school to see if I would get accepted. I had zero background or aptitude in 'academic' studying, so why try?

After two years of trying to make it as an actress, things weren't panning out the way I'd hoped, and I finally went to university. I still did not know what I wanted to focus on, so I chose a Bachelor of Arts, studying an array of languages, because I had a belief that I was good at languages and figured this would be easy for me. I also did history and an introductory course in psychology. It was only when a guest lecturer came in to PSYC 101 and spoke about neuroanatomy that something lit up inside me. I thought, *Imagine what it would be like to know all that information and to study something like that?* It sounded so exciting. Impulsively I ran down to ask him how I could study the brain in that context. Hypothetically, of course. But he told me to go ahead and change my major, so I did, and the rest is history. But to be honest, even after I discovered this passion and changed course to pursue it, I still thought that those who were high up in the field of neuroscience had something that I didn't have. I thought there was this wealth of knowledge only the gifted had access to, and I would never tap into it.

And while I am still not at the level of those academics I looked up to, I can now see that this limiting belief was not serving me. The level at which I apply myself to learn correlates directly with how I progress. And setting my sights on achieving more and more in this field is now realistic for me, as long as I am aware of the amount of work and hours of dedication that are required. Success is not due to some innate talent; it is due to application and consistency. Before, I looked at academics as a different breed, a community I'd never be a part of. I now look at myself as one and the same, just not as far up on the ladder – but getting further and further the more time I dedicate to learning.

And I feel that it is important to give credit where it is due. If I looked at these scientists and academics and said, 'Oh, they are born with this crazy capacity to retain information,' I'd be downplaying all the hard work and grit that these people have invested into their studies and careers, dismissing their success as a talent instead of what it really is: hard work, repetition, and consistency. It's not glamorous, but it is, in most cases, what's responsible for the high achievers in any field.

The same can be said for so many things – even goals we *know* how to reach. When I look at someone who is super flexible or can do walking handstands, I think to myself, *Wow, imagine being able to do that, I wish I could!* Knowing full well now that I *could* do that, in theory, and the only thing separating me from them is that these people chose to dedicate time and effort and hard work and consistency to that particular skill, and it shows. There is literally *nothing* else getting in the way. I'm not saying you have to maximise all the potential you have; maybe you have no interest in doing a handstand, and that's just fine. But we need to acknowledge what we are willing to put our efforts towards and what we are not, and then stop making excuses.

Now, let's take a closer look at learning a new skill: How long will it take you to become proficient in something? Well, you may have heard of the ten-thousand-hour rule popularised by Malcolm Gladwell, which claims you need to do something with focus and intention for ten thousand hours in order to achieve mastery. Many are not completely sure if this can be backed by enough evidence: psychologists at Case Western Reserve University conducted a new study of violinists and their practice habits, which showed how the ten-thousand-hour rule was an oversimplification. But what does seem to hold true is that the quantity of time spent practising something with intention to improve is the main factor in getting to where you want to be. This is not the same as simply doing something a lot but not trying to improve, such as driving or cooking. We all know people who have cooked for years who are not proficient because they haven't tried any new techniques, or people who have driven for decades that seem to be worse now than in their earlier years behind the wheel because they're not as careful. For some people, no matter how much they do something, it never gets better because they are not challenging themselves and trying to reach higher and higher skill levels.

This is especially important to remember when it comes to things that are more challenging at the beginner level. Most of us have no problem cooking a few basic recipes or driving around the block – but other skills are harder to even begin learning. Let's say you've always dreamed of surfing, and went out for a beginners lesson. All the students in the group managed to stand up a few times, but you didn't get even close. Would you say that you're a just-not-meant-to-be surfer? Would this turn you off from trying again? Would it be enough to make you decide that you're not good enough to ever gain skills in surfing? For many, that would be enough. You would think, *Alright, I am not gifted in this arena. Everyone who did well has a natural ability, I do not.* There are always going to be differences in everyone's first attempts: some people adapt to certain things faster. That should never be an indication of your abilities or lack of abilities. Just because the start is slow, it does not mean that you are at a disadvantage long-term. However, if you *think* that's true, then you are mentally disadvantaging yourself by throwing in the towel before truly giving it a shot.

At some point on your journey, you may find yourself wishing for something that someone else has earned, thinking 'if only'. I want you to take a look at what is really in the way of you achieving that same thing. Often it is just time, dedication, persistence, and perseverance – not much else. For most of the skills and knowledge you would like to obtain, you are in a position where you can achieve it if you dedicate yourself.

Your daily task

If you were to choose one thing, no matter how bizarre, that you wished you could get really good at, what would it be? Where could you take this new skill if you started applying yourself daily? Where do you think you would be in one month? One year? Ten years?

Now think of something that you can realistically look at improving each day or a few times each week. It can be something you're already doing that you want to level up in, or it could be something where you are starting from scratch. Ideally, I would love for it to be something that you do *not* believe you are already good at. Something that requires challenging your existing beliefs – which is an example of accommodation, which we spoke about in the first chapter. This is where you are required to modify or expand on existing thought processes, when a new piece of information is received that makes you realise you need to update or change what you think about that subject.

This is an exercise for your mind, challenging your beliefs around your abilities, more so than something to improve your practical skill set. So the activity you choose really does not matter. It can be a board game, a sport, improving your memory, a language, flexibility, how fast you solve a Rubik's Cube, absolutely anything. But for the sake of the exercise, it has to be something that you can measure objectively. And for the next three weeks, practise consistently, and document your progress. Film it, write it down, time it, record it – whatever you can do to track your progress week to week.

The key is that your practice has to be intentional and focused. Passive interaction won't really get you anywhere. You are looking to challenge yourself each session to improve. Once you start to prove to yourself that you can see progress in anything you dedicate consistent time and effort to, your ideas about what you can do will start to open up, and you will notice yourself become more creative and willing to do new things. You will understand how focused effort and intention correlate with results, and you will be able to apply this newfound understanding to anything.

1.5 What story are you attached to?

I always bang on about how bad I am at remembering names. And surprise, surprise: I never remember a name. Someone will introduce themselves to me, and I stare at them blankly, *amazed* at how fast I can forget. I say their name again in my head, and follow that with *Let's see how long I take to forget this.*

Now, this does not happen because I have a bad memory. I confidently talk about how good my episodic memory is for my own life events. Not only can I remember an event that happened years ago, but I can usually remember most of what happened in the hours leading up to the event and after it. It's just names that go in one ear and out the other. I would even go so far as to say that I have actively made this worse with this pointless narrative, labelling myself as a person with this problem.

Now let's take a look at the opposite example: I believe myself to be good at directions, and others have reinforced that by complimenting me on that skill. I can find my way around pretty easily after going somewhere only once. My father is the same; he can find his way back from almost anywhere no matter how long the trip. My mother, on the other hand, is the opposite. She will go into a shopping centre and not know which direction she was going when she exits a store. It's always as if she has never seen the shopping centre before.

When we discuss why we are so different in this way, my mother says, 'I look at street names and try to remember them, and when I come back to that place, it feels like I have never been there before.' My father and I take a completely different approach: we notice landmarks and have a visual representation rather than street names in our heads. Mind you, neither of us would consciously be noting the landmarks – it has, for the most part, been a subconscious process.

But then I thought, *If I were to* consciously *pay attention to landmarks, how much better would I be at directions and navigation?* Given that I was already pretty good at it, I thought I could get even better by putting in some effort. So I started really paying attention and noting the images of landmarks in my mind, locking them in. And lo and behold! My skills in navigating have gotten better and better, I even surprise myself.

These are two pretty common examples of how attaching yourself to narratives can be a hinderance or an advantage. In order to improve your overall mindset, I want you to pay attention to what you say you can or cannot do, even in casual conversation. How many of these things are being reinforced by what you are saying, and how many things are legitimately out of your control? You need to separate the two and start to look at the language you use around your own abilities. This kind of language influences how you behave and what you can achieve.

When you make a final statement about yourself, such as, 'I am terrible with names', 'I am too much for everyone', or 'I am terrible at making friends', you become reluctant to address or improve that. You see it as a fixed part of who you are, even if you hate it.

However, when you begin to 'attach' yourself to being adept at something, the opposite occurs: notice how much more open-minded you become. If you were to start saying, 'I'm pretty good at remembering what people tell me,' you would start taking pride in that. Because you want that to be a part of your personality and what people know you for, you consciously start putting in the effort. Instead of shutting yourself off from even trying, and reducing yourself to being as good as your worst attempt, you start to look at tiny ways you can try to improve at that skill whenever possible. It is amazing how differently you approach challenges when you change what narratives you choose to attach yourself to.

Initially this begins as conscious effort, every time. If you've always considered yourself forgetful, it won't come naturally to reverse that thought and convince yourself otherwise. But as you push yourself to reverse it over and over again, it stops feeling like such an effort, like going against what you're used to aligning with. You start to override your old patterns, until this becomes part of your new identity. Your new schema.

But I want to point out that all the examples I've given you so far are internal: beliefs about yourself that are within your control. We also need to look at external things that you may be attaching yourself to. These will also dictate how you respond to situations and challenges, and can heavily influence your mindset.

When people attach themselves to a belief, a friend group, a community, a celebrity, or a political affiliation, it becomes part of their identity. These affiliations are part of what makes them who they are. And this can provide you with something that enriches your life, such as cultural identity or faith that brings meaning to your day-to-day. But it can also hold people back. When you no longer align with the behaviours or beliefs of the people around you, you may start to feel a disconnect between the life you want to live or the kind of person you want to be and this perceived identity or affiliation.

If you are too closely attached to something, it becomes difficult to criticise that thing, group, or person. It feels like going against that entity is going against yourself. It makes debating difficult, and can cause people to react impulsively instead of creating a logical argument. This is where bias comes in. You only focus on the 'positive aspects' of those you align with and struggle to objectively criticise them even when they have done wrong. You brush it under the rug.

This, again, is due to cognitive bias, where we tend to create a subjective reality by cherry-picking the things we like about someone or something, and then ignore the red flags and undesirable traits, or dismiss them as being an anomaly. Another good example of this is when you experience something called *limerence*, thinking it is love. This is where you fall in love with the idea of someone, instead of the actual individual. You create a perfect image of them so that even when red-flag behaviour appears, you are able to dismiss it or come up with an excuse for why it happened, instead of accepting it as part of them. It goes without saying that this bias can lead us to stay in unhealthy situations and relationships because we turn a blind eye to warning signs, and before we know it, we are in too deep. Too in love to leave a relationship, too involved to walk away from a group. Not every relationship or decision should be unconditional. You should always have the ability to stay or leave, to agree or disagree. If things are unconditional, you are ultimately saying, 'I will put up with anything and still be here.'

Again, these connections are important, but creating a bit of separation between yourself and what you attach your identity to helps you become a better critical thinker. You can see the good in something, as well as the bad. And because you are not saying, 'I am this and this is me,' you can make smarter decisions for yourself. You will also have an easier time identifying when you are being manipulated, mistreated, or taken advantage of.

For example, if you align heavily with one political party, the opposing party may come up with some excellent ideas, but you may struggle to admit this, or not even be able to see how the idea is beneficial. You're also likely to defend your party when they do something that deep down you don't agree with. You might deflect or come up with excuses for why they are doing what they are doing. Ideally, you would be able to look at all parties critically and continue to choose the one that you think could do the best job. And if this means switching your affiliation every so often, that is okay. You can also agree with critics without feeling that your identity has been attacked.

I personally love listening to podcasts, documentaries, and interviews with people who were involved in pyramid schemes. I find them so fascinating, and a prime example of how people abandon logic because they become so attached to something. These people that get interviewed, who have come out the other side, became so deeply involved in these schemes, made them such a big part of their identity, that they felt they could not get out of them. This is exactly how these programs are designed to operate. Even when these people realised that not only would they never make money, but everyone they recruited also would not make money, they still stayed because they had worked so hard to make that program a big part of their life and their identity. They would make excuses for staying, and turn a blind eye to all the manipulation because they did not want to admit to themselves and those around them that it was a sinking ship, a mistake. Often, these are smart people whose identity became so attached to this scheme that all their critical thinking went out the window.

You should only ever think 'it is what it is' for things that you know are *not* within your control. In those cases, you have to find the most productive way of moving forward, despite what is happening. But when it comes to something you know you are capable of changing or improving, you can't treat it like a lost cause. That is doing yourself a disservice and under-estimating the skill set of your own brain and mind.

I would always recommend that you be quite stingy with how much you attach yourself to. This includes the narratives we spoke about earlier in this module, like *I am not a morning person*, *I am not social*, *I am not approachable*, etc., but it also applies to attaching yourself to groups of people, especially groups in which you have to live a certain way, without questioning if it is working for you.

As we reach the end of this first module, I hope you see how understanding yourself and how your mind operates is crucial to creating change for yourself in any area. There are many processes that we engage in that can go unchecked for years, which can block how we perceive the world and prevent us from changing our schema. You can attempt a goal or change as much as you want, but without understanding yourself and your habits, knowing where the blocks are and how to move past them, you will be repeating the same unsuccessful strategy when there is a shortcut to getting to where you want to be. Use these techniques to gain better insight into yourself, because you can't change what you don't acknowledge, and the more awareness you gain, the more change you can make.

Your daily task

It's time to learn to become less biased and better at critiquing things that you like – not just the things you dislike. For this exercise, write down three things that you identify with. It could be a group, organisation, fan base, religion, sporting team, brand, celebrity, etc., and give at least one or two criticisms for each of those three things. This may seem difficult to do with something you really love, but remember: nothing and nobody is perfect.

This should be an empowering exercise, proving to yourself that you can still love something and criticise it without it feeling like you are attacking yourself as well. It teaches healthy separation and allows you to make better-informed decisions.

MODULE 2

LIMITATIONS AND FEARS

It's important to know your limitations. Not so they can stop you from accomplishing your goals or slow down your progress, but so you can learn where work needs to be done, or where you need to reroute your efforts. And I want to be clear that when I talk about limitations, these are not necessarily fixed. Many of your limitations can be worked through, eliminated, or reduced. But they do require acknowledgment, and a big dose of self-awareness, as we discussed in the last module. If you learn what your limitations are, you'll know exactly where the work needs to be done to improve. You can seek resources and practise anything with proper guidance. Ignoring your limitations, making excuses for them, or just hoping they will go away will cause them to be more of a hinderance. Learning about them and tackling them will teach you not only how to improve in that area but how to tackle other challenges in a more productive way too. So in this module, I will show you how to become friends with your limitations. Do not hide away from them, because they are more powerful in the dark.

2.1 Work with what you've got so you've got more to work with.

It's time to make friends with your limitations. We want to get well acquainted, to know everything there is to know about them. The more you know about your limitations, the better your understanding of what you can or cannot do about them.

The first step in this process is learning the difference between limitations you can change and those you cannot. Take a moment to consider something that's preventing you from reaching a goal. This may be a weakness, an insecurity, or a limitation – all things that have the ability to hold you back or slow you down. First, we need to go over how to differentiate them.

An insecurity is your own perception of something that may or may not be true, and may not align with other people's perception of you. For example, you may be insecure about a physical trait and think that others notice it and judge you, but it is actually only noticeable to you. You may also think you are not good enough to achieve something a friend has achieved, despite having no measurable proof to show that you are not as good as your peer. It is a feeling or perception you as the individual hold.

A weakness, on the other hand, is a part of reality: it is not subjective. It can be something that you struggle with, like an addiction, a compulsion, constant procrastinating, or a lack of drive to get up and take action. When you think about something or someone that is weak, it's objective: for example, you can either lift a certain amount of weight, or you can't.

Notice, however, that both of these things – insecurities and weaknesses – can be changed. You can increase your strength (physically or mentally) through training, and you can face your insecurities to change how you perceive them, and eventually have them fade away. A limitation is any circumstance or rule that restricts you. So both insecurities and weaknesses could fall into this category, because they are blocks in front of you that are restricting you from moving forward.

If you are up against something you can change, then you want to be in a position of awareness, where you have studied it and you are taking productive steps to make improvements. And if you're dealing with something unchangeable, or that you cannot change in the moment, being comfortable with that limitation is an important step towards learning to be comfortable with yourself and understanding that perfection does not need to be achieved.

Let's look at another example, like one of the limiting narratives we discussed in the last module. If you have a limiting narrative such as, *I am bad at studying*, I want you to really dig deep and investigate this. Do you feel this way because you did poorly at school? Have you tried to study something you actually enjoy or are interested in? Sometimes, we tend to take an example from our past and use that to predict the rest of our future without giving ourselves another chance. But we need to ask ourselves: *Is this a fixed limitation, or am I committed to and capable of changing this?*

As a personal example, I often tell people I am not organised. But the reality is, I *choose* to prioritise other things before being organised. This is not a fixed limitation, because when I try, I can improve at least somewhat. When I prioritise being organised at the start of the day, lo and behold, my day is easier, and I can tackle my workload more efficiently. So when it comes to these internalised narratives, I want you to ask yourself: *Is it that I can't do it, or that I won't do it?* It can actually be empowering to admit that you are not willing to do something, rather than not able to do it. You are recognising that something is within your control, but you are prioritising another thing, and it's your decision to make.

That said, there *are* also limitations that you cannot change. Let's say you're not tall enough to be a basketball player, or you reached the age cutoffs for a certain sport or job. Or maybe you tried your hardest but there was still someone more prepared or better suited for a job. There are many possible limitations like this, where you do not have full control of an outcome: whether or not people like you, the weather, traffic, something going wrong that had nothing to do with you but still impacted something you wanted. And in all of these cases, it *still* helps to become acquainted with these limitations.

I have been in situations, like we all have, where I have been met with limitations out of my control, things that I could not change. I have found myself stuck in bad contracts, unlucky situations, delays on one thing that have caused a missed opportunity elsewhere, etc. And these limitations have been frustrating but also present a good opportunity to regroup and make a decision. *Do I keep trying at this thing, or has the ship sailed? Can I use this knowledge or lesson and put it towards something else?* There will be many things in life that do not go your way. But how you interpret an event will be even more important: this will determine whether you feel powerless and unable to proceed or if you can learn something from it and head in a different direction. Life is not about avoiding every bad thing or pretending limitations don't exist. It is about learning how to tackle these things in the most productive way you can, so you can enjoy your life regardless of what comes your way.

People often avoid talking about their limitations because they don't want to focus on anything negative. It's hard to get pumped up and inspired when you are going over everything you are *not* good at, or everything you have failed at up to this point. But there is a difference between self-awareness and self-destruction, between being aware of a limitation and letting that limitation define you. Acknowledging something about yourself is not the same as beating yourself up for failing. As we discussed in the last module, only when you become self-aware can you implement appropriate change.

Even though it may seem counterintuitive, there is nothing more empowering than knowing what your limits are. And the more comfortable you are with these things – the more you bring them to light – the less power they have over you, and the less people can use them against you.

There are people out there, normally not the nicest people, who will look for your Achilles' heel and try to use it against you. And if they know that a particular limitation is a pain point, then they have even more leverage. One of the easiest ways to make someone feel small is to highlight their weaknesses. But knowing this, you have the ability to turn it all around and place the power back in your hands. For example, let's say you're in an argument and you get something wrong. If someone calls you out, it feels like they were the one to discover your weakness. However, if you admit to your mistake, responding with an 'I don't know' or 'I could be mistaken,' then the power is instantly back in your hands. You are the one who knows where your limits are.

Another perfect depiction of this is when the media tries to dig into a politician's past to bring up any scandals. One photo of a politician smoking a joint or rumours of a sex scandal is enough to permanently damage their career. These are things that they try to keep buried deep down, hoping these facts or images never surface, and if they do, the amount of damage control that has to happen is wild. Why? Because the information was something that they were suppressing and hiding from. However, it doesn't have to be this way. In 1992 in Italy, a porn star by the name of Moana Pozzi decided to run for political office. She did nothing to hide her history and her career – everyone knew about her past. And while she did not win her campaign to become mayor of Rome, it skyrocketed her popularity, and she went on to co-found a political party called the Love Party, which fought for better sex education and legalisation of brothels. By owning her story and a history that some may have seen as a limitation, she maintained control of her power.

When you are the first to own your story, then not only can others not use it as power over you, but it also garners a lot of respect. That's because most people can only dream of being so comfortable with the things that they label as weaknesses. If you show that you are comfortable with who you are, people struggle to use this against you and even begin to admire you for it.

When bullies or employers on a power kick or unhealthy romantic partners try to make you feel smaller, what do they do? They will point out something that will shake your confidence. Your security. When your security is hit, you shrink to protect yourself. And by the way, people may even point out what they deem to be a weakness in you because it holds a mirror up to *their* own insecurities. And if they point something out first, making you feel smaller than them, then the likelihood of you pointing something out about them gets lower and lower. That's how bullies operate. No truly confident person, no one who is truly comfortable in their own skin, is ever going to be a bully. What I'm asking you to do is to bring your limitations to light and say, *This is me*. Let's roll with what we've got.

Your daily task

Try this exercise to help you confront your insecurities and weaknesses – the limitations we know we *can* change – as a way of minimising them. Remember, the moment you shed light on these things and stop trying to hide them, the smaller and more manageable they become. Avoidance is where weaknesses and insecurities grow.

Read the following list of statements and try to remember the last time you used one. If it's been a while, or they don't sound like things you'd *ever* say, write a few down, and see if you can apply them the next time you're up against a challenge or setback. The quicker you become comfortable saying the following, the faster you will feel comfortable in your own skin and in your own progress, and the faster you'll take your power back. Here are the statements:

1. You were right.
2. I don't know the answer to that.
3. I could be wrong.
4. I made a mistake there.
5. I will own that error.
6. I have not looked into that topic enough to form an opinion.
7. I would love to learn more about that.
8. I am not yet where I'd like to be, but I'm going to start practising this more.

When you hear someone say any of these statements, you think, *Wow, this person is self-aware and confident*. Sometimes I feel that the smartest people are the least likely to label themselves as knowing everything or being the best at something. So never shy away from these limitations, as leaning into them is the best way to teach yourself how to improve or grow, and it's a shortcut to feeling comfortable in your own skin. For me personally, the more I know, the more I realise I need to learn, and I like that ever-evolving journey.

2.2 Why do you block yourself from living the life you want?

In most normal situations, it's not something you would opt to do: block yourself from a life-altering experience or opportunity. And I don't believe we want to stop ourselves from becoming a better version of who we are, or at least not consciously. And I don't want you thinking that there's a version of yourself that is working against you and one working for you, with a constant battle going on (although it may feel like it sometimes). What's really going on is your motivated self is conflicting with your conditioned self, and this back and forth will continue until you finally tip the scales of time, attention, and habits to the new version of you versus the old. There is the concept of the future you, with all your hopes and dreams, the motivated version of you that has creative and daring ideas, which are pitted against all your learned, ingrained behaviours and emotions. Your old self isn't holding you back on purpose, it's just doing what it's been taught to do over time. And this self only does things that the subconscious mind demands of it. The subconscious mind will only ever carry out repeated behaviours that it no longer finds challenging. But this does not mean you're stuck; you can work with this and change it.

How do you become conditioned? It normally comes from either your upbringing and environment, or some major life event that has caused your emotions and behaviours towards something or someone to shift. For example, think of being heartbroken for the first time, and all of a sudden, a wall goes up and being vulnerable feels so much harder than before.

Now let's look at what is going on in the brain when this occurs. When something – a behaviour or observed behaviour – is repeated, areas in your brain undergo something called synaptic plasticity, which is the wiring or rewiring of connections between neurons. Cells that fire together, wire together. When two or more neurons fire together repeatedly, the brain will strengthen those pathways through something called long-term potentiation (LTP), which is a process of persistent strengthening of synapses (neural connections) that leads to a long-term increase in connectivity or transmission between existing neuronal synapses. It makes it easier for the brain to remember things and to repeat those patterns, beliefs, or behaviours. It is based on ongoing and recent activity and occurs in all regions of the brain, in areas such as the cortex (the outer layer of the brain, and the newest in human evolution), the hippocampus (involved in memory consolidation and learning), the amygdala (our emotional centre), and more.

LTP is very important in the retrieval of memories and emotions, and when something gets repeated enough times, or when the event is coupled with a strong emotion, the pathways are strengthened, and the event or behaviour becomes easy to remember or repeat. Emotional arousal strongly impacts how the brain consolidates memory, and when you experience moments of intense stress, fear, or excitement, you are more likely to remember the event, compared to emotionally neutral events.[1] This explains how you can become easily conditioned to avoid discomfort, something we'll talk about in even more depth in the next chapter. You might struggle to confront anything you fear if you have been taught to avoid risks, or if you find yourself simply mimicking behaviours you've already been exposed to. If no one in your family was a risk taker, you may be less inclined to take risks, or even think risk taking is a bad thing. If you were brought up in an environment where money was scarce, then your relationship with money and being financially successful would likely feel tainted and negative. Maybe when you were growing up, you saw your parent lose their job, and it became difficult for them to achieve financial stability or get another well-paying job. You noticed how much this impacted your parents emotionally, and the stress it caused them trying to provide for the family. Money was scarce and there was a lot of fear around spending too much or losing money. Whenever you go to spend money, you mimic these thoughts and fearful behaviours regardless of the income you are earning.

The most annoying part is that a lot of our conditioning and LTP occurs without us actively choosing it. Our brain experiences something and puts two and two together:

it decides, *I don't like being hurt, I don't like failing, I don't like feeling vulnerable and at risk of losing, I don't like the discomfort of working so hard at something and not doing well, I'd rather feel secure and protected. It feels familiar and safe, and it's better than being exposed and uncomfortable, so I'm going to favour things that represent safety over things that represent risk.* When you look at it that way, you can see why we can become conditioned to think in a way that doesn't actually serve us. All of this subconscious work our brains are doing is intended to protect us.

Is it your fault you're conditioned this way? Not really. Often this happens in childhood or young adulthood, when you are not able to fully control your actions and emotions. Knowing this, if you only ever listened to your conditioned self, you would seldom take a risk, be vulnerable, or try something new, because you don't want to experience pain. Is it your responsibility to change this? Yes, because, unfortunately, no one else can change what goes on inside your head.

You are not working against yourself. Instead, you are working against ingrained patterns of wiring in the brain that become beliefs. Doing something once that goes against your usual behaviours or emotions feels hard, but doing it with consistency gets easier and easier; the new ends up overwriting the old. If you create a fresh pattern and stick to it, more often than not your subconscious will follow, and you will start to feel as if you and your brain are more of a team.

The goal here is not to stop or break these wired connections. It's not about creating a void where something once was; that's too much work, and it's not even necessary. Instead, you are going to create new, stronger, and more active connections and pathways, so that the old pathways get weaker and weaker and no longer dominate your subconscious actions and reactions. Just as LTP occurs, making connections stronger, the opposite is also true. When two cells stop firing in a pattern, those pathways get weaker and weaker. You can't have two negating pathways working strongly. One will be fed and grow stronger, and the other one, by default, will weaken, because it's getting used less and less. The brain stops giving resources to that pathway to keep it strong. It's not your job to eliminate it, it's your job to pour your resources (your attention, consistency, effort) into the new pathways. Those strong synaptic connections are what become your new automatic processes. This can be done with motor skills, memories, knowledge, and beliefs. It works for logical thoughts and emotional thoughts as well.

Your daily task

To begin making a change, start by identifying what you want changed, and don't be broad; get specific. What behaviours are you done with, what emotions or fears would you be better off without? Write these down and pick the top one thing that is the most important for you to change right now. You want to challenge the habits that aren't serving you, or the limiting beliefs about who you are and who you can become. Maybe you want to change the time you wake up in the morning, or your negative beliefs around money. Maybe you want to start standing up for yourself when people put you down, or become that daring person and get your motorcycle licence, or start studying that course you always told yourself was too difficult for you. Maybe you want to become more confident in social settings and be able to have a conversation with a complete stranger without feeling crippling anxiety. Don't chose a statement like, 'I want to be more organised,' because that's too broad, and you are dealing with too many behaviours under that umbrella. Instead, you could say, 'I want to put things away in my wardrobe when I take them out and not leave things on the floor.' Simple and easy to identify. If you struggle to identify something, simplify it further until it is beyond basic. If you want to be more social, or minimise your social anxiety, you could say, 'I will introduce myself to one new person every time I go to an event.' Or, 'I will compliment a stranger on the street three times a week.'

The reason I am getting you to pick one thing to start with is that we need focused attention to make this work. When something is new, it takes effort. Your conscious mind is doing all the work, which is exhausting, and makes it easy to get fatigued quickly. Only once you've repeated it enough do you get to subcontract this task to your subconscious mind. Overloading yourself with too many conscious exercises will be setting you up for a really hard time, which might lead you to give up or think you can't do it.

When working on this plasticity and rewiring, remember that repetition is key. You are better off repeating a basic task until it becomes a part of you than struggling to do a large, complicated task. If you want to be a morning person but always wake up at 9.00 am, try consistently waking up at 8:30 until it feels normal, then raise the bar after that until eventually you can get up at the desired time. Don't start off setting your alarm at 5.00 am and hitting snooze until 9.00 am, and then kicking yourself because you now think you're a failure. Keep it so basic it would feel ridiculous not to do it.

If you're thinking of a limiting belief you have about yourself, change the wording a bit until it stops being limiting and feels realistic to you, and you can recognise it as something that you have the power to change. So, instead of saying, 'I can't speak to strangers, I get so anxious I freeze up!', instead say, 'I now say hello or smile at people I cross paths with every day.' It feels believable. The aim here is to find the first step towards improvement, not to get to the top of the ladder in one go. We need to ease the brain into changing; it doesn't love to change initially, and it can be a stubborn thing. But once you steer it in the direction you want, it will be your greatest ally, getting you what you want, every time. Simple steps are the key.

> As you do this, your brain rewires itself to get used to this new task, and the old pathways begin to weaken. And the best part is, you can rewire as many times as you like. Remember: the brain is like a muscle and needs to be trained. And just like a muscle, it responds quite well when you stick to your goal. Keep it consistent, and only after a new pattern has become a part of you, do you take it to the next step.

2.3 Stop avoiding discomfort.

Now that you know all about LTP and the way the brain forms habits subconsciously, I want to talk about why it is that we are wired to avoid discomfort. It may seem intuitive, but in order to achieve your goals, it's a habit you will have to break. I want to show you the importance of *choosing* your discomfort, given that, as I will explain now, discomfort is inevitable.

The first thing to know is that humans love to engage in a form of cognitive bias known as 'loss aversion': a psychological concept where we believe the pain of losing something is *twice* as powerful as the joy of a win. This is what keeps us living a sheltered life, scared to break out of our comfort zone. Or, as the expression goes, it's why we feel 'losses loom larger than gains'.

Because of this concept, we are hardwired to avoid uncomfortable situations or pain. This means that most people would only deal with these feelings of discomfort under threat, or because they were pushed into a corner and have no choice but to do the uncomfortable thing. Any other scenario would require a conscious decision to face the discomfort, and for most of us, taking a risk like that is not our first choice.

This is purely a protective mechanism in the brain. When you allow your instinctive subconscious mind to make all the decisions for you, they will be based around survival. And that makes sense: your brain is trying to protect you. Any form of discomfort could fall into the category of risk, so the primitive, more emotional centres of the brain will pull the breaks and get you to hesitate, think twice, and stop doing that uncomfortable thing altogether. Like anything in the brain, the more this happens, the more the brain reinforces this avoidant behaviour, and before you know it, it becomes a habit to avoid unpleasant tasks. However, when you introduce the modern, reasoning centres of the brain – the prefrontal cortex, where you have executive function and forward planning – into making a decision, you are able to look ahead and understand the consequences of your actions now, and how they impact your future. If you always listen to that default of your emotional centres of the brain, telling you to avoid discomfort, you are living in a reactive state. The more you lean into critical thinking, reasoning, and intercepting emotions with logic, the easier it is to break this built-in avoidance mechanism that we all have on some level.

So what can we do? Can we learn to take more risks?

Yes. You have the ability to train yourself to be more of a risk taker. Through a few simple tools you will learn here, you will become better at assessing risk, taking calculated risks, avoiding suffering from regret even if something does not go your way, and understanding how to capitalise on any risk you take, regardless of the outcome.

Ironically, in my life, I found that the more I lost, the *easier* it was to take a risk. Not because I suddenly had nothing to lose – there is always something to lose – but because every time I lost something or failed at an attempt to do something, I survived, and was not really worse off than before I had made the attempt. These risks didn't ruin my life. They may have ruined my immediate plans, or my ideas for the future I had created in my mind, but I was still standing, and I was fine. For me, losing things, whether it was due to my own mistakes or poor decisions, or whether it was completely out of my control, taught me how to deal with the discomfort of things not going my way.

I also realised that for almost every category in my life, when I look at failure or losing something, the fear of something going wrong was way worse than the reality of it. I thought I would not be able to move on from a heartbreak, or that I would be so embarrassed if a business idea failed, that I would never be able to attempt a relationship or a career move again. And while I experienced real pain, I also didn't crumble the way I anticipated. And I was so busy regrouping and looking at other options for myself that I dealt with these things better than I thought. Maybe not right away, but very soon after, I would be back on my feet redirecting where I was going.

The truth is, you will always face discomfort. You are either uncomfortable because you are adapting, growing, changing, learning, improving, and taking risks, *or* you are uncomfortable because you are unhappy with a certain aspect of your life, and doing nothing about it makes that part of your life worse and worse.

Health is an area where I see this subject crop up time and time again. Between conversations I've had with friends and listeners of my podcast, I have countless examples of people who are 'stuck' in a lifestyle that does not serve them. Let's say someone is drinking every weekend, which leads to violent hangovers multiple mornings a week. I would be asked, 'How can I feel happier in general, more productive? I feel like I am always playing catch-up. Why do I have so much anxiety after a big weekend out? Why is my sleep so bad? How can I turn my life around? Give me a solution, any solution, and I'll do it!'

And I ask, 'Do you really want a solution, or do you just want to feel good right now?'

Of course, they say they want the solution. So I say, 'Simple! Stop drinking.' But guess what? No one wants to hear that.

They want a quick fix. A simple action they can do to turn their life around! So I get, 'Uhhhh... is there anything else I can do...?'

The issue here is the inability to *choose* their discomfort. So many people choose, by default, the discomfort of feeling hungover instead of the discomfort of not drinking, even for one evening. And they make that choice time and time again. The same goes for being annoyed at yourself for not going to the gym in the morning. You choose the path of least resistance, never getting stronger, over the discomfort of getting out of bed earlier than desired and getting that workout in.

One reason we have these tendencies is that we always struggle to put ourselves in the shoes of our future self. It is so easy to push all the ugly stuff off for another day. Hangovers, *oh, that's a tomorrow problem*. Responsibilities, *I'll do that another time, when I've got more energy*. Difficult tasks, *I'll have that conversation next time I see that person*. Starting a new routine, *I'll wait until tomorrow, or Monday, or the start of next year once the silly season is over*. But the body does not care about the difference between Monday and Thursday. We're just fooling ourselves into thinking that there is a version of ourselves out there who is willing to do what we are not willing to do right now. What we are avoiding right now is discomfort. And the act of avoiding the discomfort *is* what will cause you to feel annoyed with yourself later on.

Annoyed you didn't tidy your room yesterday, annoyed you didn't spend a bit of time studying before your exam, annoyed you didn't stick to your morning exercise routine, and now you aren't where you want to be.

Is the trade-off worth the extra hour of sleep, or the time spent scrolling on your phone? The answer is always going to be no. And you know this. You just have to get clear on how the benefit of discomfort now outweighs the alternative, and why that matters.

I don't want you to think that everyone who has a crazy routine and works hard all the time does it simply because they love it. Or because all this motivation comes easy to them. I exercise every morning – except some Sundays, or when my body needs proper rest. Some mornings are harder than others, some mornings I get to the gym and just do a stretch, but regardless, I'm up at 5.30 am and move my body every day. And I would be lying if I said I loved it, or that I was in the mood every single morning to hit the gym. I do not love it all the time. I did not love every subject I ever studied, and I did not love all the assessments. I sometimes find creating content for the podcast more stressful than enjoyable. But I know that after it's done, I have nothing to regret, and it will make life for the me of tomorrow better and happier.

Not every aspect of your life has to be enjoyable to live a fulfilled and happy life. In fact, dealing with the unpleasant and mundane stuff is a kind of rite of passage *to* that fulfilled life. Some things you do are just a means for you to get where you want to be. If you only seek pleasure in everything you do, if you are always avoiding discomfort, you will be running away from the lessons, the challenges, and the opportunities to grow. Remind yourself *why* you are doing what you are doing, not how annoying it is that you have to do it.

So I'm asking you to pick your poison, because unfortunately you cannot live your life with zero discomfort. You are either growing and pushing yourself forward, which can be hard to do, or you are frustrated with where you are at in your life because of lack of control or drive. It is one or the other. But you always have the power to choose.

Your daily task

What discomforts are you avoiding? Come up with a list of a few things you would like to change about your lifestyle. It could be the time you wake up, how your morning is set up, how often you exercise, alcohol consumption, what you eat, etc. Then write down what discomfort you are *choosing* instead of the discomfort of following through with what you want. Noting what that thing is keeps it top of mind next time you are faced with a choice: this discomfort now, that will help me in the long run, or comfort now that will equal another form of discomfort later.

2.4 Learn the difference between pain and suffering.

As we learned in the previous chapter, I want to get you to begin to reframe how you look at the bad in your life. The things that are hurting you. They can be divided into two categories: pain and suffering.

Suffering is something that is brought on or exacerbated by you, either consciously or subconsciously. And it is something that, with practice, you have the power to reduce significantly. Yes, there are the obvious forms of conscious suffering. All of us can probably think of a moment where we *chose* to suffer. Or where we chose to dig the knife further in. Maybe when going through a heartbreak, you put on really sad music, which causes another emotional breakdown where you become inconsolable in that moment. Or maybe when you were a child and your parents got mad at you, you stormed off to your room. Even when your parents were over it and called you to dinner, you refused and sulked in your room all night, thinking it would prove something. Instead, you just sat there, pissed off and hungry. Who suffered? These are all examples of a choice to suffer, and while maybe it doesn't feel like it at the time, it was a choice, because there was a better-feeling choice on the table that you pushed away.

Pain, however, is inevitable. It is your reaction to something that has happened: loss, heartbreak, abandonment, rejection, and more. When you are feeling true pain, there is no better feeling to choose in that moment. It is a feeling that comes from within, something that is needing to be felt or expressed. This is unavoidable and should not be dismissed or ignored. Feeling your feelings is crucial, so you can learn from them and heal. Otherwise, you end up bottling them up and having them manifest in other ways.

You might be wondering: Where does discomfort fit into this? I would place discomfort in the category of pain. Because discomfort is inevitable. You cannot avoid discomfort. You can choose which discomfort you will take on, as we went over, but it will always exist. You have the choice between the discomfort of doing the hard work now or living with the discomfort of being dissatisfied with your situation, knowing change was within your power. Pain is inevitable, something to work through but not dwell on, and so is discomfort.

So, remember: suffering is a choice, pain is not. You might be thinking, *Alexis, I did not choose to be heartbroken!* Then that was pain, not suffering. I'm not trying to downplay the hardship of being dumped. But I am telling you that a lot of things start off as pain, and when we don't deal with or learn from them initially, we end up turning those feelings into suffering down the line.

For a clearer idea, here are some more examples of self-inflicted suffering:

1. Creating an internal dialogue around a situation and adding more to it than what is actually happening.

Maybe you're presuming someone has spoken behind your back without evidence, and then you end up over-analysing every interaction you have with that person.

2. Mind-reading or presuming someone else is about to say or do something that will negatively impact you. Therefore, you pull back and become defensive before anything has happened, which then creates tension and limits communication.
3. Biased thinking, or self-fulfilling prophecies. You seek out certain things that will reinforce a belief you have and therefore strengthen your negative emotions towards that thing or person or situation. For example, maybe you think that everyone is trying to rip you off, and when you focus on every opportunity where someone has tried to do so, you're not remembering all the honest, fair people you also interacted with, and then end up thinking, *Everyone I interact with is out to rip me off.*
4. Taking one negative thing that happened and applying it to all these other areas in your life. Let's say someone criticises how you do one thing, so you start to think of all the things you must be bad at, or that you are likely to fail at.
5. Intentionally reminding yourself of something that caused you pain. Maybe you've been guilty of reading over texts or old cards from your ex when you are trying to get over them, causing you to take a few steps back on the progress

you've made, and you feel your emotions begin to spiral all over again.

6. Blaming yourself for things that were not and never have been in your control.
7. Digging for information that you know would hurt you, especially information that you don't know exists. For example, searching through your partner's phone for evidence of cheating or any hint of bad behaviour. This could lead to looking at how they worded a text message and interpreting something friendly as flirting and inappropriate. Then you feel like you have to be on alert in case your partner is cheating, causing you to want to search through their phone even more.
8. Looking at one behaviour in somebody and presuming they must be angry with you, not taking into account that there are many things that could have upset this person that have nothing to do with you.

There are tons of examples, but by now I'm sure you're sensing a pattern. One habit that really leans into that self-inflicted suffering is mind-reading and spiralling thoughts. We can create the most elaborate narratives in our minds about what other people are thinking or feeling, why someone has been watching your social media even though they dumped you, and reading into every text message and every action. We will ignore what is being shown to us in words and behaviours, and clutch at assumptions instead, spiralling into thinking of the worst-case scenario. When you are in the thick of one of these spirals, it does not feel like you have control. But sometimes, the simple act of identifying what is happening is enough to reduce or eliminate these thoughts.

My mum used to tell me a story that explained what happens when you presume what others are thinking. It is also a story we can all apply to our own lives in some way, as most of us have been guilty of mind-reading and catastrophising.

The story goes like this: A man wants to borrow a guitar from his mate. So he leaves the house and starts walking down the road to his friend's house. Along the way he starts thinking, *What if he says no? What if he makes up an excuse not to lend the guitar to me? That would be annoying, because I've lent him things before, so that would just be so unfair. He'll probably come up with some stupid excuse and make me look like a fool for asking. He is just going to make it uncomfortable and embarrassing for me.*

The man continues walking, getting closer and closer to the door, and his demeanor has now changed: he is worked up and annoyed. He starts to think even more. *Now, I'll have to walk all the way back home with no guitar because he cannot be stuffed lending me something. He would never do something kind for me no matter how much I do for him!* The man keeps creating all these different scenarios in his head of what his friend will say, and what excuse he will give for not lending the guitar.

He finally arrives at the door and knocks, almost furious now. The friend answers the door, happy to see him, greets him politely, and in a rage the man blurts out, 'You know what? You can shove that guitar up your ass.' And he storms off.

This is a prime example of how we cause ourselves suffering with mind-reading: we presume an outcome that is not in our control. And even if that does end up being the outcome, we're forcing ourselves to experience it beforehand and allowing it to ruin our mood. How simple do you think it would be to change that, and to look at a situation with a more open mind?

Sometimes we will suffer but tell ourselves we are actually 'protecting ourselves'. For example, say you really want something: a job, a date with a crush, to invite someone to some event, to borrow something, to get time off work, etc. But you work yourself up, trying to read their mind, thinking you will be mortified or embarrassed if it doesn't go your way. You go back and forth, round and round in this mental loop, wanting to avoid the pain of rejection. But what is really happening here? You are causing yourself suffering. By avoiding pain, even just the potential for pain, you suffer. Pretty ironic.

The same goes for actions that you do or don't take, as we discussed in the discomfort chapter. By avoiding the pain of getting up early to exercise, you suffer later on, because you are annoyed you never invested the time to train your body. By avoiding the pain of hours of dedication and sacrifice, you never did that course and got that job you dreamed of. Every avoidance of one form of discomfort or pain leads to a different kind of suffering. What is easy now will make it harder for you in the long term, and what is hard now will make your long-term goals easier.

Back to that guitar story. My mum would tell it to me and say, 'The worst case scenario is that they say no, so you may as well give it a go.' It's no use presuming the outcome. You could be shutting down opportunities before you even knew there was an open door for you to walk through. And if they say no, are you any worse off than you are right now? No. The only difference is that you were sitting in potential, but nothing was being actualised anyway.

This is a lesson I wish my younger self learned and put into practice a whole lot earlier when it came to crushes or situationships. When I was younger, I would be 'seeing' someone, but deep down, I would feel like it was going nowhere. And instead of asking point-blank if we would take it further, I would just wait for them to initiate a hangout, and cruise along for weeks or months, never wanting to ask. I thought this was protecting my feelings because a rejection would hurt, but in hindsight, investing time and energy into someone that doesn't like you back hurts way more than rejection ever could. I would have saved myself a lot of time, frustration, and tears, instead of just cruising along hoping it would eventually become what I wanted it to be.

Always remind yourself that pain and suffering are two different things. And if something results in pain (receiving an answer you do not want to hear, ending a relationship you know is not right for you, trying something you know you are not good at), you now understand that it will happen sooner or later. Pain is a teacher and cannot be avoided. Suffering can be let go of, because these are the behaviours that you choose to engage in, with no positive outcome. Once you can see examples of both things in your life, it becomes easier to differentiate the two, and easier to let go of behaviours that bring you suffering.

Your daily task

Choose one or two specific scenarios in your life that you are avoiding. Maybe you are afraid of an outcome that will cause you pain, so you do not engage. You do not ask that person if you can date exclusively, you do not ask for time off because you do not want it to be rejected, you do not go for the things you want because you are scared of a negative outcome.

It's time to change how you approach these things you fear by deciding which pain you will choose: the pain of being brave and going for what you want, risks and all, or the pain of not getting what you wanted because you never took the risk.

> Get clear on one situation in your own life where you can be bold, and go for what you want or need with no expectation. This will show you how liberating it can feel to push past the suffering of spiralling thoughts and fear by taking back control and allowing the situation to unfold. Even though you cannot control everything, you can control your own efforts. These efforts are often uncomfortable, but necessary for change to happen, or for you to receive an answer you need.
>
> What will that thing be today or this week? If it scares you, that's a sign that you're on the right path.

2.5 Choose a growth mindset over a fixed mindset.

By now, you've already seen how easily influenced your subconscious mind is by certain statements. Remember how telling myself I was bad with names made it even worse? And telling myself I was good with directions made it even better? Now we're going to take it one step further and get you excited to start making some changes in the way you speak to and form your beliefs about yourself. In this chapter, you will see how we can change how we approach challenges by simply changing how we speak about them. This begins from a very early age and influences how quickly you give up on something, or how many times you will attempt it. It also frames how you perceive your own intelligence, and how you view failure.

Psychologist Carol Dweck created a body of research around the topic more than thirty years ago, and much of what she and her team discovered still rings true today.[1] They focused on young students and how they approached failure. They wanted to know why some kids would be so affected by failure and setbacks, while other kids seemed to bounce back from failure easily and unaffected. Dweck coined the terms 'fixed mindset' and 'growth mindset' to describe what was going on here. It turns out that it all comes down to the beliefs that people have regarding their own intelligence and ability to learn, no matter their age.

A fixed mindset is when you believe that your human traits, such as personality and intelligence, are 'fixed', or unchangeable. When you feel that these things are fixed, that means that where you are at now is the limit of your abilities, and there can be no further improvements. And because of this belief, failure becomes something you avoid and fear. You try not to make mistakes, and you don't want to push yourself too close to your capacity, because your only options are hitting a ceiling of what you are capable of, or 'failing', which a lot of people do not want to face. This then leads to taking less risks in life and having less experiences and opportunities as a result.

A growth mindset is believing that these traits in your personality and intelligence *can* be changed, improved, and developed with time and effort. If you believe that your skills can improve the harder you work at something, then you are not only more likely to put in the effort when you come across a challenge, but you are more inclined to take on challenges, learn from your mistakes, and not shy away from failure. This is because you do not see failure as final but as a stumbling block on your journey of growth and improvement. You recognise that the more effort you put in, the more growth you have, and failing, falling short, or hitting a plateau is just part of the journey. It does not sway your confidence in your abilities, it just highlights which areas need more work.

Dweck also realised that children with a fixed mindset gave up more easily, felt threatened by the success of others, would perceive criticism as an attack, would avoid hard work and challenges (as these could end in failure), and felt the need to prove their intelligence to others. Children who had a growth mindset looked at criticism as a chance to improve, were not overly affected by negative feedback, and looked at others' success as inspiration. They would want to engage in challenging activities to help them improve, but also didn't feel like they had to be proving their abilities or intelligence.

If you are listening to this and thinking, *Oh no, I think I have a fixed mindset*, no need to worry! This is a limitation that can absolutely be changed, and I want to tell you about another recent study that'll show you how.

In 2017 a paper was published called 'The "Batman Effect": Improving Perseverance in Young Children.'[2] It explains the benefit of something called 'self-distancing', which is where the individual takes an outsider's view of their own situation. In this study, young children were asked to do a repetitive task for ten minutes, with the option to rest and play fun video games instead, to test their perseverance. They were split into different groups, and one group was told to pretend to be a hardworking fictional character – someone they looked up to, like Batman. The group who pretended to be Batman persevered the longest. When children saw themselves as a superhero, their overall perseverance went up.

This nods to the fact that when people get out of their own heads in this way, the pressure of having to prove themselves is alleviated, and they are more likely to keep trying. Instead of frustration or negative thoughts getting in the way, simply pretending to be someone else is enough of a distraction from your own mind to get you to put in more effort, and therefore achieve better results.

By disconnecting in this way, the person has not changed, but their attitude did. All of this is to say: it is up to you to change how you approach things. You may just need a bit of a shift in how you approach challenging situations and failure.

This Batman study helps explain how someone can shift from a fixed mindset to a growth mindset by changing how they perceive a situation. You may be someone who puts a lot of pressure on yourself to achieve perfection in everything you set out to do. Breaking out of this may seem impossible because you are set in your own ways. And the idea of growth mindset that I spoke about earlier may sound great, but it doesn't come naturally to you. When you shift your perspective, take on another character, or imagine being someone else, it allows you to attempt something in a way that maybe you have struggled with in the past, based on your own beliefs about yourself.

Going back to Dr Dweck, she also found in studying children's mindsets that something as simple as changing how people encouraged students helped guide how they tackled a challenge. Rewarding children for their effort made kids work harder and take pride in their work, even more so than in the end result. Praising a child for their innate talent or stating how smart they were had the opposite effect.

So, what can you take from this? How can you apply these scenarios that work in children to your current situation? Do you resonate with fixed mindset or growth mindset? Both may be true for you. And you can swap over to a growth mindset at any time, and this way of thinking can be applied to anyone at any stage. Adults are just a little more hardwired in their ways, so we need to work harder to consciously make a change.

Like I spoke about in the 'Change how you look at your capabilities' chapter, if you believe there to be a ceiling to what you can achieve, if you think that there is a predetermined level that you will reach, then the way you approach things will reflect that limitation. What if you didn't know what the limit was for yourself?

When I look into my future, I purposely try not to flesh out exactly what I want to achieve or be doing in five or ten years' time. I just have certain things I want to work towards, and I'm always seeing where I might be able to take it next. I keep my long-term goals based around health and relationships, but I always try to leave room in my consciousness for career and creativity; that way, I'm often pleasantly surprised with how things unfold for me, and I can lean into things that are going well. And for the things I end up finding more challenging, I am not held back by my expectations around how long it should take me to master something or achieve a particular benchmark.

Additional resources

If this is a subject that interests you, the book *The Alter Ego Effect*, by Todd Herman, is all about the power of finding the hero inside each of us. It builds on the ideas presented in the Batman study and shows how every one of us can benefit from thinking of our identities in this new way.

2.6 Dealing with regret and wasted potential.

No one wants to live a life where they look back and think that they have wasted their potential. But before we can understand that phenomenon, we need to understand what potential actually is. Potential is messy, it's undirected, it's unpolished, and it's a novice at everything. It's the *I 'could' do something.* In every life, there are endless possibilities for careers, relationships, and experiences. And as we go through our years, we make more and more selections that cut out the possibilities of other things. We buy a house, we choose a partner, we invest our time and energy into certain activities over others. That is how it is supposed to be; it is the only way it can be. So we will all get to the end of our lives knowing that we had the potential to do things that we didn't do.

In my opinion, this idea of wasted potential rarely comes from thinking you chose one path over the other and messed up. It more often comes from a lack of action in general; when you didn't *actively* choose any path but rather went down the path of least resistance. Or there's this feeling of reacting to what comes instead of being proactive with your decision. You ended up pursuing the career where you felt confident enough in your work but never felt that it challenged you. Or you ended up coming home from work and sitting in front of the TV or on your phone until dinnertime every day. Then you look back in twenty years' time and think, *I wish I had gone for walks, or played indoor soccer, or learned a new skill.* Or *I could've spent more time with my best friend or my partner or my dog.*

The subject of potential so often comes up around people's careers, but it does not have to be this idea of quitting the nine-to-five and starting your own business and becoming your own boss, blah-blah-blah. Some people love to have set hours, love to work for a company, love to be part of a team. Not everyone needs a hustle or a side hustle. So this is not restricted to career. It could also be what else you did with your time.

To me, real wasted potential is not wrong choices, it's lack of action. The more you pacify and procrastinate, the more you risk feeling you have wasted your potential. It's knowing that you *could* have done something but didn't do it, for no good reason. If there was a real reason why you were not able to do it, then it would not have been wasted potential. It was not a choice; it was a real limitation that you bravely learned to accept, like we discussed at the beginning of this module.

You might be thinking: *But what if you don't know which path to choose?* The classic issue of analysis paralysis. The feeling where there are many options in front of you, and you are not particularly compelled to choose one over the other. Possibilities are pointless if you don't follow through with at least one of them. If you stay somewhere waiting to feel a certain way, waiting for the right thing to find you – the perfect job, the perfect hobby, the perfect moment – you could easily watch life pass you by. And only in hindsight will you look back and think, *I wish I studied architecture!* Or, *I wish I learned to play the guitar! I had the time, why didn't I do something with it?*

To put it simply, the antidote to feeling like you have wasted your potential is to just start on something. Do not wait to be hit in the face with passion and excitement, or for your instincts to scream 'This is the right thing!' Just take action. Most of the things that worked out for me didn't feel exactly right at the start; I just thrust myself into it, kept chipping away, and hoped for the best. Like I told you, I threw myself into acting, which wasn't the right path for me, but it led me in a roundabout way to my true passion for neuroscience, not to mention how many times I tried to start my own blog or business on the side only to have it fall flat on its face. But the point was that overall, there was progress, and it felt good. I'm always glad I tried.

Now, we can't talk about potential without talking about its number-one enemy: the idea of being 'too late'. That feeling is one of the biggest killers for an idea or a passion or a curiosity. And it's a total lie.

How many people have started something later in life and completely transformed their career? How many people have changed their lifestyle after decades of following habits that were not working for them? You could want to start something new for five years but always talk yourself out of it for it is 'too late' – yet had you started that thing back when you were originally talking yourself out of it, where would you be now? Hundreds or even thousands of hours of applied focused time, versus still waiting to take the first steps.

When it comes to potential, I would also encourage you to think deeply about your role models. Who are you looking up to? Who inspires you? When you look at others who are doing what fulfils them, do you feel a pang in your heart that you cannot have that thing, or is it a spark showing you that it is now possible for you? Be very picky with the people that you surround your awareness with, whether on social media or your real-life mentors. Make sure they make you feel that they are an example of what is possible for you. If you are not inspired by those around you, if you feel old when you look at what others are doing – no matter your age – change your landscape and find better examples.

And there are plenty out there! Here are just a very small selection of people who have made something happen for themselves at an age when most people wouldn't dare try. Use these people, or find some new examples of your own, every time you are about to say, 'I'm too old,' or, 'It's too late.' It's up to you if you are too old, no one else.

Julia Child didn't release her first cookbook until the age of forty-nine.

Alan Rickman was a graphic designer before he pursued acting and didn't land his first big movie role until the age of forty-two.

Vera Wang didn't become a fashion designer until she was forty years old; she was a figure-skater, and then spent more than fifteen years in journalism before launching her first collection.

No one is exempt from changing. Either you will create change, or the world will change around you. And often, it is the people who have been through the hardest adversity that end up creating the greatest change, because their circumstances compelled them to do so.

Sometimes you will get too comfortable. Sometimes you will stay on one path even if it is not working for you because you feel you have invested too much into it already, that it would be a 'waste' to change course. This is actually a psychological phenomenon called the sunk-cost fallacy. This thought process causes you to continue to invest time and money into something after a loss has already occurred and the investment cannot be recovered. This can be applied to gambling, a career, a course of study, or even a relationship where no one is happy but you stay together because 'it would be a waste to break up now'. You could finish university and already hate the career you chose, but because you invested the three or more years of time and money getting qualified, you stay working in that field for *decades*, wishing you had an entirely different life or chose something else. But the longer you stick with something that's not working, the greater the loss will be.

If you are faced with a situation like this, it is important to ask: What am I truly gaining by staying? If I stay doing this thing, will it actually recover the loss? If the answer is no, then ask: Am I choosing to stay because I do not want to come to terms with the loss, and staying in it makes me feel like it's not all lost yet?

Feelings of regret can be an even bigger source of pain than failing at something. And that's because regret is a reflection of what was in *your* control; you had a choice. You cannot regret something that was not in your control; that is not possible. For example, if you try really hard to get a job somewhere and you miss out in the very last round, no matter how upset you are, it's not something you can truly regret; you gave it your all with the resources you had. The rest was not up to you.

Hindsight is all fun and games, but the truth is, it doesn't help in many situations. Personally, I don't even think the term 'regret' should be used for things that you thought were a good idea at the time. I remember after facing a few heartbreaks and really struggling emotionally, I would say I regretted meeting that person and regretted dating them. If I had never met them then, I would not be experiencing this pain now. But of course, after some healing, it was clear that it's not a regret I should carry with me, because at the time, I thought this person was great. There were happy times before the sad ending. How was I to know any different? No one has a crystal ball, so to regret this kind of thing is to cause yourself unnecessary suffering.

Reserve regret for the times you went against your instinct or didn't take action when you knew you should. And then *do something* with that regret. That's right: you can make regret useful. To sit there and beat yourself up about all the things you didn't do with your time and knowledge is not serving you in any way. Instead, use this intense emotion to learn a valuable lesson, then at least the feeling of regret will not be in vain. In my times of deepest regret – which are normally when I did not stand up for myself or walk away from something I knew was toxic, or the times I said no to a potentially unforgettable experience – I use that as an example to my future self. I say, 'Thanks for that feeling, now I know exactly what to do next time.' And I can peacefully move forward. I'm not sitting in regret but moving past it with more knowledge of myself.

Your daily task

How can you turn your regrets into lessons? Think of something you've regretted in your life, and what that feeling of regret has taught you. Has it taught you to be more present with the people you love? Or to take care of your body and mind more carefully? Or to treat your next partner better? Or to choose the experience over money? When you can identify a lesson, then the regret has been of use. And it's not all bad.

MODULE 3

RELATIONSHIPS

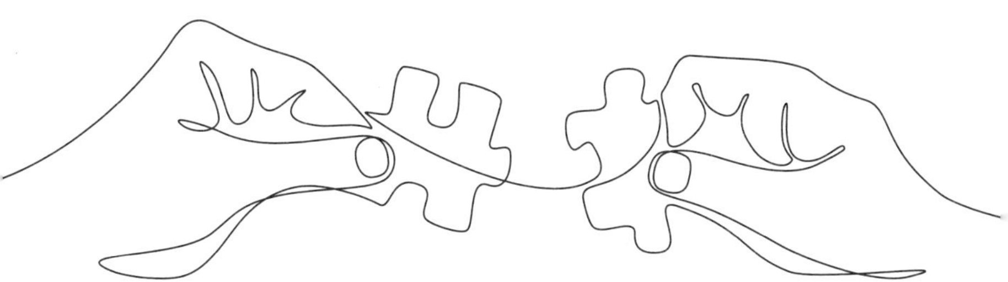

Welcome to module three, where we'll cover all different kinds of relationships. It is impossible to go through life unaffected by your relationships with others, or only focusing on yourself. Humans are social beings, and feeling part of a community is a basic need that we will always prioritise. However, this is also why we spend so much energy seeking approval and validation from external sources – another subject we'll get into here.

So far in this book, I've been talking about your journey as an individual – how to get to know yourself better, and to overcome fears and limitations. Now it is time to bring in one of the most important factors in our lives: our relationships, because the quality of your relationships has a huge impact on the quality of your life. We'll start with your relationship with yourself, and then get into your relationships with others. This module will cover everything from how to set boundaries, how to nurture healthy independent relationships, how healthy relationships contribute to your successes, how you can overcome challenges in your relationships, and more.

3.1 Your relationship with yourself determines the quality of every other relationship.

If there is one thing I want you to take away from this book, it is the importance of your relationship with yourself. The way that you treat yourself will be the benchmark of what you accept from other significant relationships in your life. There may be some people who come into your life and treat you even better than you treat yourself (bonus!), but there is always a risk that others will treat you as low as the bar that you have set. And if that bar is too low (or there is no bar), then you are at the mercy of someone else's standards. And that is simply not good enough, if you want to have high-quality, fair relationships. So let's talk about how we can stay in control.

Your relationship with yourself is the foundation of all other relationships; it's the base they're built on. Only when you have that solid base where you can lean on and rely on yourself do those other connections remain solid. If you lose yourself to relationships, to poor mental health, or to work, then every part of your life will suffer. However, if you work on yourself consistently, and hold yourself as your number-one priority, then everything won't be affected when one area of your life is challenging, because you have not lost yourself.

So look at your relationship with yourself as your insurance policy, the one non-negotiable. It's easy to prioritise work commitments and other people ahead of your own needs. However, when you understand how you need to show up in every area in your life, you will realise nothing can and nothing does come before this.

Now, where do we begin putting this concept into action? Putting yourself first can manifest in many different ways. So if you're not one to run a bath, light some candles, and have alone time, keep reading, because there are even stronger ways of showing yourself love and respect. Some examples include:

1. Keeping a promise to yourself
2. Creating boundaries – something we'll discuss in-depth in the next chapter
3. Sticking to a habit in order to achieve a goal
4. Dedicating time to a self-focused task
5. Saying no, or not allowing someone to treat you poorly

Every time you show up for yourself, defend yourself, or keep a promise, you are saying, 'I matter to me, and I deserve this level of respect and treatment.'

If you're not sure why this is so important, it may be helpful to think about some of the things that can go wrong when we fail to prioritise our relationship with ourselves. When you break a promise with yourself, for instance, you are saying, 'I can't count on myself, and there is something that is more important than me right now.' And the more times you break a promise, the less conviction you have each time you set out to do something, like embarking on a new goal or challenge. It could even get to the point where your word means nothing.

And if your word means nothing to you, then how much respect do you have for that part of you that is supposed to have your back when no one else will? This is where we begin to rely on others to keep us accountable, or to make us happy, or to make us feel validated. When we are not used to following through for ourselves, we seek that assurance somewhere else. And what happens there? We feel let down and hurt when people don't meet our needs, when a lot of the time, those needs could be met by us first and foremost.

Relying on others for the self-worth and motivation we need gets dicey very fast, because beggars can't be choosers. Sometimes you'll get lucky, and have good people come into your life to support you and lift you up. But other times, not so much, and you will have people who let you down. The pain of being let down by someone else is never as difficult to bear if you are there for *yourself* when times are tough. However, if you are not, this pain becomes unbearable, and your ability to trust others gets damaged in the process.

Trust is another thing that will become a lot easier for you when you become your own best friend. It is so much easier to trust others when you have trust in yourself first. You are saying, 'No matter what you do to me, or how much you hurt me, I will be okay and I will be able to heal from it, because I am the constant in my life.' When you cannot love yourself, respect yourself, or prioritise yourself, the thought of someone breaking your heart or abandoning you can be one of the most terrifying things to be confronted with. That's often why people stay in unfulfilling relationships or why they put up with unhealthy treatment. Because the fear of being alone feels terrifying. But the truth is: you are enough.

Think of someone you know right now who is that kind of person. Who commands respect. Who is comfortable in their own skin and who is not afraid to say no or defend themself or even just walk away from a situation they do not feel comfortable in. One of my favourite examples in pop culture is Rihanna, who is always comfortable speaking her mind or defending herself calmly during red-carpet interviews. Even when questions seem annoying or offensive, she is able to defend herself, and put someone in their place without being rude and without getting offended. She clearly knows her worth and doesn't need to seek validation from others in these moments.

And if you have ever asked yourself, *Isn't all this self-love kind of selfish?* It is important to know the difference between the two. Self-love, beyond doing nice things for yourself, is about prioritising your primary needs. You are making sure that your needs are met (physically and mentally) by doing things such as having alone time, standing up for yourself, or removing yourself from an unhealthy situation, protecting yourself, and giving yourself the things that fulfil you such as purpose, adventure, and security. When you are the only person who is directly impacted by a decision you make, it cannot be a selfish decision. *Selfish* would be putting yourself above other people who would be impacted negatively by that choice; for example, making a decision for yourself and your partner that benefits you, but disadvantages them, or expecting others to drop everything for you but not doing the same in return. Or maybe it'd be expecting other people to listen when you talk, but always cutting off those other people when they try to speak. These are all examples of being selfish, not practising self-love. If you are minding your own business, it is not and cannot be selfish.

And when you love yourself, you will never fear being alone again.

Your daily task

If you don't know where to start with showing yourself love and strengthening your relationship with yourself, begin the day with a very simple task. Make a promise to yourself. Start with one you know you are able to keep. It's not about challenging and testing yourself right now, we'll get to that later. Right now, we are just laying down the foundations with something simple.

The criteria for this promise are:

1. Something you know you are capable of doing and have done before (for example, going to bed by a certain time, or not drinking alcohol today)
2. Something that you don't already do consistently (so it represents new effort)

Examples of this might be:

1. Drinking a tea or coffee in silence early in the morning, before you talk to or message anyone
2. Meditating first thing in the morning
3. Waking up fifteen minutes earlier than you normally do, and journalling/checking in with yourself
4. Carving out thirty minutes for reading fiction to wind down in the evening, with no distractions

None of these things is unbearable, but they do require you to carve out time just for you. And the simple act of doing this makes you feel like you are worth it. It is a positive loop that keeps feeding itself. Choose one thing, and if you succeed, see it through for the next seven days. And if you are sitting there saying, 'Alexis, seven days is a lot in a row! I can't do that,' then you need to simplify the promise even more. When it comes to making permanent and lasting changes, less is more, and the long game is better than the short.

3.2 Setting boundaries is the key to better relationships.

What is a boundary? A boundary is where you determine the limit is for how someone will or will not treat you. It is personal, it is about protecting yourself. The key here is that we are *only* addressing behaviour directed at you. Setting a boundary is saying, 'I will not allow you to do this to me,' not 'I will not allow you to do this.'

For example, a boundary would be that you will not tolerate being screamed at. Let's say you have a colleague with a tendency to raise their voice, and you explain that if someone wants to communicate with you, it has to be done calmly or in writing; you will no longer be yelled at. That is a behaviour that directly impacts you, and that you are not willing to put up with. If that line is crossed again, you remove yourself from the situation. And when the other person can communicate calmly, you can resume talking to them.

Boundaries are all about expressing how you feel clearly and being able to remove yourself from or not engage in a situation that feels unhealthy, unsafe, or unfulfilling. However, this is *not* about making demands and requesting that people do certain things to serve certain needs. It is about what you are willing to expose yourself to. It is about your autonomy – not about controlling and manipulating others.

I want to be really clear about the difference between setting a boundary and trying to control someone's behaviour to suit your needs or wants. Proper boundaries are very important, but some people like to request something from someone else and justify it by labelling it as one of their boundaries that needs to be respected. However, when unchecked, this can become pretty unhealthy, and even lead to situations of coercive control in a relationship.

Let's say your partner is hanging out with colleagues from work, and you say that because you don't like these particular colleagues, him spending time with them is crossing a boundary for you. This would actually be attempting to control your partner under the guise of a 'boundary', because the act of him hanging out with someone else does not directly impact you. You not trusting someone to spend time with others is not under that person's control, and therefore does not fall under the category of a boundary. Similarly, a partner telling you that dressing a certain way is crossing one of their boundaries is just a way to justify controlling behaviour.

Think of an example of a boundary that you have set in the past. And now think of a time that someone crossed one of your boundaries. How did you react or respond to that? Did you respond? Or did you just feel ignored and upset? If you are someone who has had their boundaries crossed on numerous occasions, then you want to look at restructuring how you set up your boundaries moving forward. We want them to be solid and to protect you, instead of letting you down and leaving you feeling frustrated. Here are some questions that will help us do just that.

The first question you want to ask yourself when setting a boundary is: Does your boundary have a consequence?

Most people only do half the task of boundary setting, and that is stating where the line is. But they never even contemplate the very likely scenario of what it would look like if someone does not respect that line and crosses it. Whenever you set a boundary, you want to have a very clear idea of what the consequences will be if it is crossed. A boundary with no consequence is not a boundary. It is wishful thinking or simply a desire. You need to think of the worst-case scenario, because there is a reason you are setting that boundary in the first place. It is because it needs to be there. And if it needs to be there, you need to have a game plan for the day it gets crossed.

This leads us to our second question: What is a healthy consequence?

Given that boundaries are all about protecting your own space, and not manipulating others' decisions and actions, the best consequence is to remove yourself from the situation if possible. Remember: you are not out to punish someone; you are protecting *yourself* and teaching others how you expect to be treated. Walking away, getting off the phone, turning down an invitation, not responding to a particular comment or engaging in a harmful conversation: these are all appropriate ways of making that line clear, without forcing someone else to act. Best-case scenario, they will notice you retreat and edit their behaviour so you feel comfortable again. If they do not change their behaviour, then you have two choices: create some distance between yourself and that treatment, or resign yourself to putting up with that treatment. You can always ask someone to treat you with respect, but you cannot force them to do it. In that case, it's not genuine, and it will never last.

This is the difference between commanding respect and demanding respect. Commanding respect shows that you are in control of the situation you are in; demanding it shows that you are, in fact, not in control.

Another thing you'll want to ask yourself is: Is the consequence of crossing this boundary *consistent*?

Keep in mind that it is your responsibility and no one else's to uphold your boundary once you set it, and consistency is important. If one day, you give a consequence for how someone speaks to you, and the next day you don't, then people may try to push the limits, and it gets difficult to maintain consistency.

That's not to say that bad patterns can't be broken. You may be wondering: What about existing relationships? If you are trying to lay down new boundaries in an existing relationship because you no longer want to put up with a certain behaviour, this can still be done, no matter how much history you have with the other person. Every single relationship can evolve and be improved as long as both parties are committed and willing. If this is your situation, it's important to have a conversation with this person about why you no longer want to receive a certain level of treatment or be exposed to a particular behaviour. Make sure you choose a time when you are both calm to have this talk. If you're in the heat of an argument, the importance of what you are saying may be diluted.

And, by the way, I don't want you to get stuck thinking that people around you are crossing these lines with you because they are innately arseholes. People have conditioned ways of being and form habits based on what they deem to be acceptable or unacceptable. We all have our own set of standards, and we are responsible for protecting those standards. If your auntie is always body-shaming you every time you visit, but you never create a consequence for her, then she is going to think that it may not be 'that bad', or that because she was always exposed to it, it's okay for you to be.

Now, what if someone asks you *why* they need to change their behaviour towards you? You do not owe anyone an argument nor an explanation to set a boundary. You do not have to explain why you need to protect your space; if someone cannot see how a behaviour can be hurtful to you, it is not your fault or your responsibility. For me, if the conversation is calm, I'm always willing to give someone an explanation.

But if someone is being pushy or aggressive, I keep it simple and remind myself that less is more.

While any kind of relationship can benefit from healthy boundaries, from family to coworkers to friends, I find that romantic relationships are often where people struggle – myself included. I once found myself feeling stuck in a relationship where I had put this person on a pedestal. Because of this dynamic in my relationship, I found it really difficult to say no, or put any boundaries in place. Whenever I did try to establish a boundary, this guy would throw a tantrum and turn it around to make me feel I was being unreasonable. I began to lose confidence that what I wanted was fair to ask for – not being yelled at during arguments, for example – and this ultimately led to me allowing him to walk all over me and determine the outcome of pretty much any disagreement. My fear of setting a boundary was actually just a fear of the inevitable: the relationship coming to an end. I was not prepared to walk away from him, and that is why I could not set a proper boundary. I knew deep down that he would never respect the boundary, and my only option would be to have the relationship break down. Had I put boundaries in place for what I was not willing to put up with, the relationship would not have made it past a month.

People will learn very quickly what you will and won't put up with simply by observing how you respect yourself and how you set boundaries. And you will notice that certain people who used to mistreat you no longer appear in your life. They're no longer there to talk down to you, make fun of you, or disrespect you. They are just gone. Why? Because unfortunately, people who do that look for easy targets. When you are no longer easy to manipulate, they move on to someone else. It's like animals in the wild. If the target appears too strong, the predator won't bother attacking, as the risk of failing is too big. They just move on to the next target.

When your confidence is shaken, you put up with unfair situations. Maybe you think you won't find a better relationship anywhere else. You think being alone is the worst-case scenario. But once you start working on your relationship with yourself, and carving out healthy, respectful relationships with others, you will value situations where people don't make the cut, because it saves you so much time. If someone is not willing to respect a boundary to make you feel comfortable and secure, then they are not meant to be with you on this journey. The more comfortable you get with that idea, the easier it is to wave goodbye to the people that are not right for you, instead of sacrificing your self-respect to keep them in your life longer.

Your daily task

Have a look at your current relationships and the boundaries you have put in place. Scroll through texts, emails, or your call log to consider who you're regularly in touch with, and how you're communicating with each other. Are there proper boundaries in place? Are they repeatedly being crossed? And if so, what will you do moving forward that does not require manipulating someone else's behaviour but respects the boundary?

Remind yourself that no matter who the person is, no one has a golden ticket into your life where they can treat you how they want with no consequences. Only you determine that. You have the power to change that. No matter if they are a partner, related by blood, or anything else. No one is entitled to that.

3.3 Manage your expectations for your relationships.

What makes a healthy relationship? Whether we like it or not, and whether we realise it or not, relationships – especially those we choose to enter into as adults – offer up a value exchange. We stay in relationships with people because we value them, and we get something out of that connection. If you were the only one giving in the relationship and you were getting nothing in return, you would get sick of it pretty quickly. It would make no sense. That said, it's not about tit for tat: it's more so a dynamic where both parties win.

I'm sure you can think of examples of lopsided relationships, where one person does everything for the other. One of the biggest red flags I like to warn my podcast listeners about is partners who are constantly reminding you how much of a 'catch' they are. I once found myself on the receiving end of this kind of dynamic, always being told by my partner that he was a catch, that he was so good, and did so much. And in hindsight, I realised this was often said whenever *I* had done something good for the relationship. It was his way of evening the score in his mind.

As social beings, we innately want to feel like we are getting value and giving something of value to those around us. That it is a fair exchange, not an unfair power dynamic. However, a fair exchange does not mean total reciprocity. Remember how I told you in the last chapter on boundaries that you can't control another person's actions, just their treatment of *you*? I want to dig deeper into that idea of letting go of that control, which is the key to managing your expectations of those around you.

Not everyone thinks about or processes things the way you do, shares your morals, or behaves the way you would behave. Therefore, how you treat others is not an exact indication of how others will treat you. So to expect particular behaviours from others, especially when that's not the way they normally behave, is to set yourself up for disappointment.

It is very easy to find opportunities to be disappointed if you look for them. People are constantly unintentionally disappointing other people simply by existing, because they're not living up to some unspoken idea that someone else had in their head.

This way of thinking is known in psychology as the 'false consensus effect', also referred to as the 'consensus bias'. It is the tendency for a person to think that their own opinions and beliefs are typical or more common in other people than they actually are. Basically, it's when someone's thinking that the general population shares their view. And the less you encounter people who dispute or challenge your point of view, the more this bias is confirmed.

Because of this, you are more likely to project your ideas as the right ones, and when someone acts differently from what you believe is the correct way, you think they are wrong or flawed, instead of seeing their opinion as one that's as valid as yours.

You can see how this can set you up for disappointment. Instead of seeking to understand how others operate and why, you assume the worst about their behaviour towards you. You need to consider that not everyone values or sees things the way you do. It helps you feel less attacked when someone reacts a certain way, and it helps you process when someone does something to you that you would never do to them.

This also means that you need to limit the amount of people who owe you. Nothing leads to feelings of resentment, powerlessness, and frustration faster than when you feel like something is owed and you are not receiving it. It is very restrictive and unpleasant and throws you into focusing on negatives, or that something is unfair, instead of feeling proactive and empowered.

I'm not saying that no one can owe you anything, but keep it to a minimum, especially when it comes to emotions and actions. Feeling like you are owed an apology, an explanation, closure, owed a favour because you did one for someone else, or owed a gift or invitation because you offered one first – these can all be ways of creating suffering for yourself, when the alternative is far more liberating.

In many cases, someone may *think* they apologised, or gave you a proper explanation or closure, but you were left feeling like it was not enough. Who suffers? The other person is off living their life, as they do, and you are left festering and ruminating over something that someone else may never think about again, because they think it has been resolved.

You should be very selective with what you need from others, and if someone is exiting your life (for example, an ex-partner), then try not to need anything from them at all. When you feel like something is owed, that person holds the power. And until they give you what you need, you cannot move on, or heal, or forgive, so you are putting yourself in limbo. This can be soul destroying, needing something from someone who does not even want to be in your future.

I remember my first heartbreak. I felt so emotionally betrayed because I was not given a reason. It just ended abruptly and coldly. For more than a year, I would repeat the same story of 'I never got closure, so it's hard for me to move on.' This impacted how vulnerable I allowed myself to be (not very) and impacted how much I could trust others (not much).

After a year or so, I was really starting to get sick of my own narrative. It was repetitive and annoying, and, most importantly, nothing was changing for me. Telling this story over and over to whomever would listen did not make me feel any better. If anything, it made me more annoyed, like I was completely powerless. I was telling myself, and anyone who could be bothered to listen, that I was waiting for this missing piece so that I could move on, and until that happened, I would not be able to heal. Meanwhile, my ex had moved on, was doing things with his life, probably not ever sparing much of a thought for me waiting for closure. He had well and truly moved on to a new chapter in his life. I was the only one suffering in that dynamic as I waited, scorned and bitter, while the world just kept turning.

It gets to a point where you need to think, *Is this a realistic expectation, knowing what I know about this person? And what is more important, my peace of mind, taking control back, feeling like I am the one in control of how I feel? Or making sure that person lives up to* my *moral standards* (whether they agree or not) *by giving me what I think I need from them?*

The longer you persist and insist on putting the power of your healing and moving on in the hands of someone else, the longer it will take for you to seize control of your own circumstances. Remember what I told you about your relationships with yourself being your foundation: don't rely on others for what you can provide all on your own.

And to be honest, the breakup was not all bad. Moments like these act as great learning opportunities. I sometimes like to imagine times where others may have expected something from me, and I either did not know about it or did not value that same thing enough to worry about it. Regardless, I fell short of their expectations and unintentionally let that person down. It is humbling and helps me see things from other people's perspectives – even the perspective of my ex, who I never spoke to again! It helps me become more understanding. It reminds me that we all have our own thing going on, and that so often you can work yourself up about something that another person will never see the way you do.

To start managing your expectations, I want you to offer a clean slate to every new relationship you get into, whether it's professional, romantic, or friendship. Create your expectations of that person based on their behaviours or their track record. If you've never seen this person give a gift, don't be disappointed when they show up empty-handed to your birthday party; maybe they show their love in other ways.

A healthy relationship begins with healthy expectations. From now on, unless someone gives you reason to believe otherwise, try presuming that they do not think exactly like you do, and therefore do not react to certain situations the way you would. They may value and perceive things in a different way. It takes away the feeling that every disappointment is personal or intentional, and helps you to see that it is all part of human interaction.

Common courtesy is not common. But as long as you know yourself, know your boundaries, and give the people around you the space to be themselves, you can set the right expectations for every relationship in your life.

Additional resources

For today, I want to share some resources you can check out if you would like a deeper dive into managing expectations to improve your relationship.

Firstly, I'd recommend taking a look at John Gottman's work at www.gottman.com. He's a psychologist and an expert on relationships. This whole website is filled with great articles, and I'd particularly suggest 'The Truth About Expectations in Relationships'.

You could also check out episode 74 of my podcast, 'Letting go of unrealistic expectations to improve your relationships'.

3.4 Understand the value you provide and receive.

I want to expand further on something I touched on in the previous chapter. That is the idea of a value exchange within relationships: a dynamic where both parties are receiving and giving value. This is a rule that all healthy relationships should follow. And to do that, you need to know what you bring to the table and make it clear to those around you.

One way of looking at a value exchange is in the 'throw and catch' of conversation. If you're having a conversation with someone where you are asking all the questions and their responses are all one-word answers, the conversation gets tired very quickly, and you lose interest. If you are in a relationship and your partner tries to connect with you by asking you a question, commenting on something, or making a statement, and you ignore them or answer without looking up from your phone, how would that make your partner feel? And how do you think they would feel after the tenth time, trying to create a small moment of connection? You can live in such close proximity to people yet be so disconnected, because you are not engaging in this throw and catch of communication. You may not be seeing the value they are trying to bring, and therefore you're not adding to it, you're letting it fall flat on the floor.

Let's go over a few scenarios to really bring home my point about the importance of a fair value exchange, which applies not only to partners but to family, friends, and colleagues as well.

A few years back, I had a job where I worked my ass off. I always covered shifts, put in the hours, and got great results. However, I felt uncomfortable when my employer would bang on about how lucky I was to have that job. It was annoying, because while I had always been grateful for my employment, I did not feel like anyone was doing me a favour. I had earned my place there through effort and hard work. And being told over and over that I was lucky to be there insinuated that my employers were offering me more than I was offering them.

One day, I had pretty much had enough, and I decided to say something. After my boss said something about how lucky I was to be there, I responded, 'Do you feel that I am not fit for the job?' By the way, I knew I was performing well at this job. He was pretty confused by my question and said *of course not.* So I explained to him that if he thought I was so lucky to have this job, it seemed like maybe there was someone out there who was better qualified for it. I was grateful for the opportunity, but I was not going to be made to feel like someone was doing me any favours by employing me. He never made that comment again.

If an employer is always making out that you are lucky to have the job you have, you may want to ask them what they feel you should be doing to be adequately deserving of the position. Alternatively, you could ask them if they think that you are not doing what your job description states. Because if you are, then it is an even value exchange. No one is doing anyone favours here. You offer a unique skill, or your time, or both, and they pay you money in exchange.

This may feel less clear-cut outside the workplace, but the concept of a value exchange still applies. In friendship, if you are eager to hang around a particular group, but you are always bossed around, told what to do, are the butt of every joke, etc., then you are likely in a dynamic where you are made to feel that you are lucky just to be there. Therefore, they can treat you how they want, knowing you will stay. (Mind you, I use the term 'friendship' loosely in this context, as that is not how I would describe a friendship.)

This is how bullies operate in high school, but you would be surprised how often I get emails from adults still experiencing this in their 'friendship' groups. I can guarantee you, if you find yourself in this dynamic, there is not much you can do to get them to change how they see you apart from walking away. People always think having no friends is the worst-case scenario, but if your friends are treating you this way, you are already *in* the worst-case scenario. You are better off going it alone and opening up space to truly find your people.

This is why it's so important to know what we bring to the table before we request certain things of others. If you feel lucky to get the attention of your peers or friends, it's hard to ever request anything from them – even just their respect. When you are in a healthy, close relationship with someone, you have mutually earned that status in each other's lives. And if you look at all the closest people in your life, and the relationships with longevity, they are the way they are because you both provide and receive a lot of value. Maybe not at the same time, maybe it comes in seasons, but overall, your connection serves both parties significantly. This is to say, in a healthy partnership, there will be times when one partner needs to be supported and does not have the capacity to give; they may be going through a hard time, are sick or fatigued or burnt out. And this is where the other partner can come in and try to pick up the pieces. Each person feels supported and secure and is then able to offer the same in return when the roles are reversed. It is not always fifty-fifty all the time. That is the kind of support that makes people want to continue to invest in each other; not measuring tit for tat but, instead, wanting to invest when they can, and accepting help and support when they need it.

Which brings me to my last example of romantic relationships. Psychologist John Gottman, the relationship expert we discussed in the last chapter, researched couples for decades to try to figure out what makes a romantic relationship successful.[1] He arranged for a large group of newlywed couples to attend a retreat, and he observed how they interacted. They engaged in activities like cooking, eating, relaxing, listening to music, and just hanging out together. He found that all through the day, partners would make requests for connection, and he referred to this as a 'bid'. A bid can be any gesture or comment to engage with the other, such as, 'Look at that sunset,' or 'Can you hold the door for me?' And while the actual subject might not be of significance, it demonstrated that the partner was looking for a response from the other. This bid for a response is how couples try to connect with each other, even if for a moment over something small.

When a bid was made, the other person either 'turned towards' their partner, where they responded and engaged, or they 'turned away', where they either dismissed, responded with the bare minimum, or ignored their partner. In some cases, their response was hostile, and they were annoyed that they were interrupted from what they were doing.

Gottman discovered that these bids impacted marital wellbeing. Six years later, the partners who had divorced were found to have only 'turned towards' and accepted each other's bids 33 per cent of the time during the initial study. So seven out of ten times, their bids were ignored or dismissed. Those who were still together at the six-year follow-up had a much higher average 'turn towards' rate at 86 per cent of the time. Nearly nine times out of ten, they were engaging in connection when the other partner was seeking it.

With just this simple observation, Gottman could predict the success of these couples years down the line. It ultimately comes down to how the couples give and receive connection. When one person needs to connect, how does the other respond? By contributing with kindness and thoughtfulness, or with the bare minimum? This is the value exchange I'm trying to show you.

Manipulating this value exchange is how love bombers operate. If you have found yourself in this situation, you know how difficult it is to crawl out of it. And if you've never heard the term before, love bombing is a form of emotional and psychological abuse disguised as flattery. The love bomber goes above and beyond to manipulate you into falling in love with them at the start, but once your guard has dropped, and you are comfortable in the relationship, feeling in love, the behaviours then change into controlling, jealous, and manipulative actions.

Love bombers aim to manipulate you in the long term. They will initially bombard you with favours, gifts, experiences, treating you in a way that makes you feel amazing. Once you get used to receiving all this, it feels like you could never compete, repay, or rival the incredible things they have done for you. They get you to a point where not only do you feel lucky to be around them, but you also feel indebted, because you could never repay them. It's hard to believe someone like this exists, as if you have hit the jackpot. And once they have you hooked, they take everything they have done for you at the start of the relationship and throw it in your face. You will forever feel indebted, and when you raise an issue in the relationship, they invalidate your feelings by reminding you how much they have done for you. You feel like you do not have a leg to stand on, even though you always should. And this is how you slowly end up in a very one-sided relationship, where the love bomber holds all the power.

Now, I don't want this love-bombing example – or anything else I've told you in this chapter – to make you feel like you can't ask those around you for anything. Accepting favours is perfectly fine when you need them, and from people who have your best interests at heart. And when it comes to offering a favour, only offer if it is truly a favour, one where you expect nothing in return. Are you willing to give without receiving something in exchange? If so, go for gold. But expecting to be repaid for something you offered to do is another way of causing yourself suffering.

Remember, for the most part, you are not exchanging the same thing, but you give something of value, and you receive value in every relationship. This is how healthy connection works. If you feel that you are always indebted to others, it becomes difficult to ask for what you want or need, and it places you in a powerless position. You feel like you get what you are given, and you do not feel comfortable asking for more. When there is an even value exchange, you ask for what you know you deserve, and you don't feel uncomfortable doing so. You know what you bring to the table. Don't look for favours, look for where you can add value and therefore ask for more value in return.

You should feel grateful for your close relationships, but you shouldn't feel 'lucky' in the sense that it's a fluke that you have this in your life. You either deserve it, or you don't. If you are a good partner, a good friend, and a good employee, you deserve that respect back. Own it. Understand you have earned it.

Additional resources

If you want a deeper dive into love bombing, here are a few resources where you can learn more:

There's a great article by the Cleveland Clinic: 'What Is Love Bombing?': https://health.clevelandclinic.org/love-bombing

I'd also recommend a YouTube video by psychotherapist Terri Cole: 'What is Love Bombing? Narcissistic Predator Alert': https://www.youtube.com/watch?v=YL7dPef3eGU

Or, you can check out episode 91 of my podcast, 'Love bombing – How to identify it and how to run for the hills.'

3.5 Maintain your autonomy.

Autonomy is paramount to any successful relationship. Each of us has a need to feel that our choices and actions are self-directed, as opposed to feeling pressured by others. This is one critical element to that relationship we have with ourselves, which we discussed at the start of the module.

So, what is autonomy? Autonomy is the ability to self-govern. It is the self-determination to make your own decisions without being controlled by anyone else. It is being able to behave in a way that aligns with your morals, values, and desires in any situation. And I want you to be able to see how increased autonomy in relationships helps form stronger bonds. If you and your partner or friends have control of your own lives, it allows for the relationship to evolve and for you to develop naturally alongside each other, in a way that works for each individual.

A study published in 2019 by Kluwer et al.[1] discussed the importance of autonomy. It explains that those who have autonomy within their relationship feel a strong sense of wellbeing. This then encourages them to want to engage in behaviours that are beneficial and positive for the relationship, which ultimately keep the relationship healthy.

The paper talks about autonomy and relatedness as basic needs, and shows that when both these needs are met, it allows relationships to be maintained in a healthy way. 'Relatedness' means a sense of belonging, intimacy, closeness, and attachment. The study emphasises that autonomy actually predicts conflict response in couples, because it leads to improved social interactions and better coping strategies. Those with high levels of autonomy are more supportive of their partners when conflicts arise.

Now, let's consider what happens when we enter a relationship without autonomy, or we lose it along the way. When you are controlled by another, or when you need to get approval from another to do whatever it is you want to do (seeking validation for your ideas), then you may find yourself in a position where you are easily swayed by their opinions. Eventually you begin to rely on them and their judgement to feel like you are doing the 'right thing'.

Let's look at examples of decisions that you should be able to make without needing input from others, no matter who the other person is.

1. What you choose to do in your spare time
2. Who you choose to spend time with
3. When you want to say no to something
4. How you spend your own money
5. What you choose to do for a job/career
6. How you dress/your style
7. What you believe in (such as religion or spirituality)
8. How you treat your body (routines, exercise, diet)
9. The hobbies you choose to do

If you find yourself in a situation where either a) you are being controlled in one of the areas on this list and do not have the freedom to make these decisions for yourself, or b) think you are entitled to tell someone else what they can and cannot do in these examples, then there is an uneven power dynamic at play in this relationship. Instead of coexisting and growing together, these are patterns of control. This can lead to the breakdown of a relationship, one person eventually resenting the other and feeling like they never lived life on their own terms, or simply feeling like they never had control over their own life and decisions. Think about the phrase 'the old ball and chain', which can be used condescendingly to refer to a partner. That was clearly created by someone who felt they had little freedom and autonomy in their life.

Notice that this list does not include decisions that should be made *together*, as a couple, for instance. Decisions that directly impact the other person, such as living arrangements, rules around what kind of relationship you want (monogamous or otherwise), how joint funds are spent, how you treat someone else's time, and honouring commitments and promises, can and should be made together. That is all separate to this chat about autonomy, because teamwork and compromise are crucial when two or more parties are involved in the outcome of a decision.

No matter how much you love someone, if you feel like you have not been able to live the way you wanted to and have the freedom to make choices about your life, it will negatively impact that relationship.

Another sign of a lack of autonomy is fear of entering relationships because you don't want to lose your independence. Some people feel protective and therefore keep their walls up, avoiding getting vulnerable with someone else. Or, once they're in a relationship, they mourn their single life. Often it's not actually that they miss being single, with the freedom to sleep with anyone on a whim, but, instead, they miss the scale of independence they had over their own life, how they chose to live it, without having to answer to anyone. However, a healthy relationship with solid foundations should not take that feeling of owning your own life away from you.

Remember: relationships are there to enrich your life, not to detract from it. But if you are entering or rushing into a relationship or friendship out of need, or fear of being alone, then you may find yourself caught in this dynamic where you lose this sense of freedom. This is why it's so important that any connection is built on that solid foundation of your relationship with yourself. Control over yourself equals less of a need to control others in your life.

You might be wondering: *Why would anyone try to control someone they love?* People who try to control those around them do so because they feel a lack of control over their own circumstances and their lives. This is why there is so much control in co-dependent relationships. A lot of people will fixate on controlling the things they have no control over, for example, people and circumstances, instead of focusing on what is really within their power, like their behaviour, language, actions, and feelings. They think their issues stem from external sources instead of from themselves, so they fixate on that. But with self-awareness comes an ability to turn around the things that are not working for you. You don't need to control those around you to feel safe, validated, or content.

Another reason that many people try to control these factors in their partner is because they do not want their relationship to change or end. They try to keep the other in a mould that works for them, that serves their needs, or aligns with their morals. They use tools such as guilt to prevent their partner from exploring and expanding into other areas of their life. These controlling behaviours normally stem from insecurities and anxiety, and are often learned behaviours from what this person has been exposed to growing up, or what they have experienced in previous relationships. But remember: no matter what's happened in the past, every partnership or friendship follows its own set of rules. So just because someone is used to behaving a certain way, it does not mean you have to put up with it too. You set your own rules together.

And here is the clincher: change is inevitable. Whether you embrace it or suppress it, there is no way of stopping change.

If you fight it, you will have a horrible time in the process, and once the change has inevitably occurred, you will have a hard time accepting it. If you embrace it, you allow yourself the possibility to love this new chapter, to discover something different and new and to allow for more change within yourself. It is a choice you have every single day: to embrace the inevitable, or to fight it.

So, what about your relationship with family members? It can be hard when you would like to improve your relationship or set some boundaries and stand up for yourself with someone you've known an entire lifetime. It feels difficult to make change with people who know you so well. But the rules for friends, romantic relationships, and colleagues also apply to your family. Just because someone is related to you does not mean they are exempt from the standards you're setting here. You may need a bit more patience in teaching your family how to treat you moving forward, because adapting to change can take a while, but you can and should establish where you would like the relationship to go; for instance, not accepting being made fun of, comments about your body, being guilted into feeling you have to follow a career that makes your parents happy, feeling like you owe your parents for bringing you into the world, etc.

Some people are stuck in the most unhealthy family dynamics, but feel they have to keep the peace because there is a bloodline there. I want to be clear that *no one* has a golden ticket into your life. People have to earn their place there, just like you earn your place in the lives of those you love, and you do this through respect, care, compassion, and understanding. When you feel unsafe, attacked, or unloved, you do not have to stay. You should never be guilted into putting up with treatment that is damaging to you.

As we've been learning throughout this module, relationships serve to create a partnership; they give you an opportunity to grow and change alongside another person who supports you, has your back, and is there to share in the good and difficult moments. If you ever feel worried or scared to ask your partner about something you want to do instead of excited to share with them what you *will* do, this is an indicator that maybe you don't have as much autonomy in your relationship as you need. Autonomy is not to be confused with detachment, by the way. You can feel connected and have a healthy attachment to your partner, and still feel like you have free will and are in control of your own life and decisions.

Moving forward, I want you to ask yourself if you are happy with the level of self-determination you have in all of your relationships. And if not, which areas do you wish you had more freedom with or control over? When it comes to making decisions for yourself, you should always feel empowered and in control.

Your daily task

Ask yourself: How much do you do for just yourself that does not include or impact anyone else? Do you have hobbies or interests that you engage in just for you? Or, alternatively, do you seek to do everything with other people, like your partner? As we spoke about earlier in the identity chapter, it is easy to get our identity wrapped up in other people, or to do things simply because you are around others a lot and their influence rubs off on you. But how much of what you do is done for yourself, to tap into your own interests and passions?

I want you to find one or more things that you can do that have nothing to do with your partner or friends. An activity, hobby, a ritual, a special walk you do that only you know about; something to strengthen your independence and relationship with yourself. The more you do this, the easier it will be to find autonomy in other things, and it then makes it easier for you to want the same for your partner, friends, and family.

3.6 How to deal with losses and move forward with vulnerability.

I know that just going by probability, many of you reading this book right now are going through the pain of a heartbreak or a relationship breakdown. And if this is not you right now, you have likely been in this position at some point in your life or will be in the future. Pain and loss in life are inevitable. You need to know how to deal with pain when it happens.

Pain does not destroy you. It forms you. And as you already know, the way that you learn to deal with it will determine *how* it forms you. You can be burned by it, or you can be fueled by it. Pain does not exist to ruin you. It serves as a teacher; it forces growth when you otherwise would have been too scared to do so. It creates new avenues for your life, and you gain more wisdom than you ever could have if you had not experienced it.

This again circles back to the growth mindset versus fixed mindset conversation we began in module two. Those who feel they have to live up to a certain level of intelligence or giftedness are less likely to take risks. They struggle with failure, shut down when something does not go right, and do not attempt anything they think they will fail at because they don't want to taint the image that they hold of themselves. They are scared to lose. Those with a growth mindset do not focus on the wins or losses. They are more process driven, they look at mistakes as an opportunity to learn or grow, and they expect to come across at least some hurdles in order to get to where they want to be.

You can apply this to any area in your life. And if you have a growth mindset when it comes to relationships, you can be more secure in how you approach outcomes, especially when something doesn't go your way. You understand that there is only so much in your control. You cannot live your life trying to ensure that your partner will not leave you, or that nothing in your life will change. Instead, we are going to learn how to live a life where you deal with pain in the most productive way possible and view it as an integral part of the human experience. You can start saving that time spent in heartbreak and waiting for closure, for situationships to turn into relationships, and for explanations from friendships that didn't go the way you wanted them to.

When you hold onto something too tightly, you suffocate it: friendships, romantic relationships, and more. I have learned this through many failures in my life. The first time heartbreak happened, it was horrible. I felt as though it would turn me off wanting to date or trying to put myself out there ever again. But once I recovered, I realised everything was actually fine. I was still here, and other good things had happened along the way. I was a lot better off than I had predicted I would be. Eventually, instead of dreading the same experience, I would approach putting myself out there in a new way, with true vulnerability. I would think, *Well, I made it through the last one, so what is the worst that can happen now?*

What does vulnerability mean in this context? It basically means to be exposed. Open to the good things, and also the bad. For example, in a conflict setting, vulnerability is being in a position where you are exposed to being attacked or harmed. In a relationship, it means you are exposing yourself to potentially getting hurt emotionally. In order to gain real connection, it is imperative to show and share vulnerability. And one of our highest values is connection. It is one of the greatest human needs. When we have it, a large part of us feels satisfaction with life. When we don't, we suffer.

The reason that many people avoid being vulnerable is because they don't believe they could cope if things went wrong. But the mistake these people make is believing that you cannot get hurt if you do not show vulnerability. The truth is, staying guarded doesn't stop you from hurting. Just because you do not show it, you still feel love, you still care, you're just only showing a small side of it, and not benefiting from what vulnerability could bring you.

Even after the heartbreaks I've been through, the way I approach my relationship now is from a position of being vulnerable. If I do the best for my partner and my relationship, I have done all I can do with what is within my grasp. Spying on my partner, controlling him, checking in on what he is doing, seeking reassurance that he is doing the 'right thing' constantly will definitely not increase the likelihood of him wanting to stay in the relationship. It does not foster trust and would likely push my partner further away. True vulnerability comes from understanding that you are choosing to love this person knowing that you cannot control the outcome. It is trusting someone without all the answers. It is not punishing the people in your life now for the mistakes of people in your past.

If you give a relationship your all, and it ends anyway, I want you to walk away with your head held high. This is a *great* opportunity to focus on your relationship with yourself. If being alone with yourself or your thoughts is the worst-case scenario for you, then of course you are going to hold on tight to what you have, even when it's clearly not working. It's acting out of desperation. Now you know better than to place your partner on a pedestal, and think you are 'lucky' to have them. If you build on your relationship with yourself and you truly know what value you bring to the table, you can approach a new, healthier relationship with openness and vulnerability.

When you underestimate yourself, the prospect of loss or heartbreak is terrifying. While it is painful to lose a relationship that is important to you no matter what, when you love yourself, you understand you are capable of having more of the same. This shift in how you approach loss makes it less scary. You no longer live in fear that something will fall apart; you live in the knowledge that if something does fall apart, you will be able to pick yourself up, and other things will come your way.

Always remind yourself: 'As long as I have myself, I will ultimately be fine.' The more you allow and the less you force, the happier your relationships and, in turn, your life will become.

Additional resources

To learn more about vulnerability, I would suggest listening to:

- Brené Brown's TED Talk, 'The power of vulnerability': https://www.ted.com/talks/brene_brown_the_power_of_vulnerability
- Episode 81 of my podcast, 'Breakup and Heartbreak Hacks to move on'

MODULE 4

DISCIPLINE

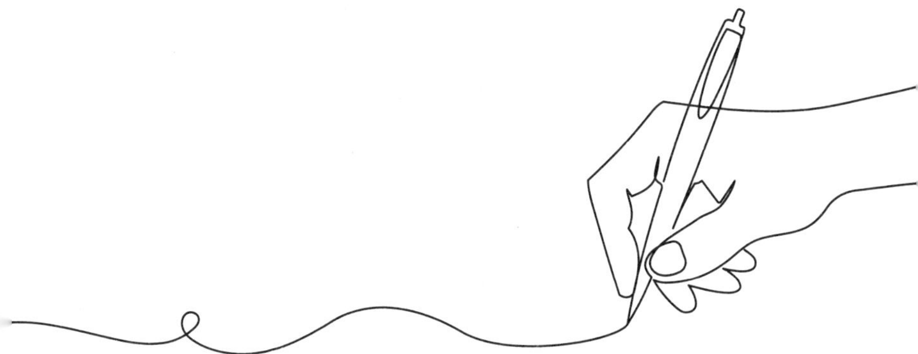

The word 'discipline' may initially bring on thoughts of feeling controlled or being restricted, but in this module my goal is to get you excited about incorporating discipline in all areas of your life. The truth is, mastering this will help you achieve levels of freedom that you currently do not have. This module will have you reframing the concept of discipline, and seeing how you can easily incorporate it into your life in new ways. Without any other changes to your existing resources, becoming more disciplined will give you more time, adventure, happiness, money, and more.

4.1 What does it look like to understand and have command over your mind?

When I think about having control over the mind, the first step is self-awareness, as we covered in module one. To know your mind, to understand how it works, its strengths and weaknesses, is to be able to change it. Awareness of the self, and identifying what is within your control versus placing control in the hands of others, will go a long way in helping you gain command over your mind. You cannot change what you don't acknowledge. I hope that everything we've covered so far has helped you achieve this higher level of self-awareness.

Once you are armed with this self-awareness, the next key ingredient is accountability. Most people don't even realise how often they give up control to other people and things outside of themselves. They live their life feeling like a victim to their own circumstances, unaware of how different it could be if they changed how they thought about hardship and hurdles. Examples of giving control to others include a lot of things we've discussed in previous modules: seeking closure from someone who cannot provide it, and therefore being unable to move on or heal; holding a grudge until you receive an apology, and not being able to stop thinking about how you have been wronged; waiting for permission or validation to feel okay with making a bold decision; waiting for everyone to agree with you before you feel comfortable to express yourself; telling yourself that the reason other people are successful is due to luck, or something beyond their control.

I cannot stress enough how important it is that you stop doing this: handing over control of something that you yourself could be taking care of. When you do this, you not only voluntarily strip yourself of control over that thing, but this action also impacts your confidence in making strong decisions for yourself later on. The more you cede this power, the lower your ability to trust your own decisions. The more you lean on others for validation, for answers and for permission, the more you place blame on others when things don't go your way. Sometimes your biggest fear when making a decision is knowing that if it goes pear-shaped, the responsibility falls on you. So you end up staying in this place of inaction.

Remember, like attracts like; the more you do something, the easier it becomes for the brain to perform that same task again (whether you think it is a good thing, like a healthy morning routine, or a bad thing, like procrastinating or engaging in addictive behaviours). So, while it may seem like a huge effort at the start because you are not used to doing something, the more decisions you make for yourself, the easier it will become to harness your power in the future. Just like a muscle, your brain is being trained to be able to make independent decisions and follow through. And once you get used to taking action, the thought of something not working out will no longer paralyse you, because you realise it is all a numbers game. As long as you are always taking action, you will keep improving, setback or no setback.

However, that accountability is crucial; when something goes wrong due to a decision you make, you need to be able to own it. It is the price you pay for control over your life and command over your mind. You take the wins with the losses, and you get to own not only your mistakes but also your successes.

If you make up an excuse for every single loss you've had, blaming other people, feeling like someone let you down when they promised they would help, blaming the weather and other circumstances, then it's going to be harder to feel like you have control the next time.

And it will also make it harder to really own your wins as a result of your own hard work. If you think everyone around you who is successful simply had good luck, then you are saying that success is luck and therefore not in anyone's control. Yes, there will always be people who are more fortunate than you. However, I find it more empowering to know that others have what they have due to effort, because effort is something everyone can do; it makes success seem more possible. It is empowering to give credit where credit is due, and it expands your awareness on what can be done in your own life.

Being self-aware and accountable for your losses does not have to be a daunting task. As we discussed in module two, there is a difference between accepting ownership in loss or failure and putting yourself down while assassinating your own character. Just because you are honest with yourself does not mean you have to be damaging your relationship with yourself. On the contrary, it's a skill to be able to pull yourself up and honestly say, 'I was not as prepared as I could have been. I see how prepared my competition was, and I can learn from them.' Or maybe, 'That job was just not the right fit for me,' instead of assuming the person hiring was an arsehole. Doing this kind of tough but fair reflecting teaches you that not succeeding does not have to interfere with the respect you have for yourself, that your missing out on something does not mean you won't be able to achieve other things or that you are not good at what you do. It teaches you how to move forward and what to do the next time you are presented with an opportunity or challenge. Without this accountability and reflection, you may unintentionally repeat the same errors that you never acknowledged in the first place.

Most people learn a lot more from their losses than their wins. Why? Because if you are always winning, you are not exactly sure what the formula for success really is. You never have the chance to correct, edit, redo, and study your own behaviour until you're able to change an outcome. And if you always fear losing, then you will always avoid taking bigger risks, because you don't know how to cope with the failure or the loss.

A lot of people ask me about 'accountability buddies', which is the idea of sharing a goal or commitment with someone else who's on board to keep you motivated and on track. Where do

I stand on this? Personally, I think accountability buddies are the icing on the cake. They can make goals a bit easier to achieve and fun along the way. However, these buddies should *not* be solely responsible for getting you to take action. Make sure if you have one, you are not leaning on them for everything, expecting them to do more work than you do, or blaming them for not doing enough to motivate you.

And when it comes to your romantic partner, think very carefully about getting them to be an accountability buddy. This works for some people, but when one slips up, it can be easy to blame them for not getting you up early, or for offering you a piece of cake late at night when you promised you would both quit sugar. You begin to get annoyed and resent your partner for not living up to the expectations you have placed on them, and this can cause unnecessary tension. At the end of the day, the buck must stop with you, and the longer you use accountability buddies (or anyone else!) as a crutch for why you have not succeeded, the longer you will feel powerless, when in reality you hold much more power than you give yourself credit for.

If you put your own personal growth in the hands of someone else, then you will never feel in control of the trajectory of your life. If you make a commitment with someone to embark on a challenge together and they slack off or give up, it is not your cue to do the same, and it is not productive to blame them for not helping you. If the help is there, take it, but do not rely on others to transform your life and your relationship with yourself. Everyone is on their own journey, dealing with their own shit. Make sure you don't relinquish the power you have to change your situation because someone broke a promise. You are your own accountability buddy first and foremost.

Being self-aware and being able to own what went right and wrong will transform you from a reactive person into a proactive one. You see what can be changed, and this then makes you feel in control of the situation, leading you to take action. So never avoid taking accountability and looking at your mistakes, flaws, areas for improvement, and downfalls. These are your guide to the lifestyle, routine, and physical and mental health you seek.

Additional resources

For more on this subject, I'd recommend the book *Grit,* by psychologist Angela Duckworth. In it, she argues that innate talent is not the key ingredient to success but the effort you put into achieving your goals, and your ability to persevere through challenges.

4.2 Adherence and self-efficacy will help you stick to your goals.

To truly chase change, you want to start taking a holistic approach to how you grow and develop on this journey. We're evolving emotionally, physically, mentally in relationships, etc.; we're looking at everything. To do that, we need to ensure we're setting realistic goals for ourselves along the way. And when I talk about making goals realistic, I don't mean you need to dumb down the goal or make your dreams smaller. I mean that you have to consider: Does your goal fit in with the lifestyle you truly want? It's all well and good to have a goal in one area, but do other areas of your life align with your ability to maintain it?

If you like the idea of being a competitive bodybuilder, for instance, but your life revolves around social interactions, and eating out with friends and family, then this is going to be a much harder task to adhere to than it would be for a homebody who doesn't really drink or like to go out for meals. What I'm telling you is: you don't have to resist your lifestyle that brings you so much joy. Instead, find a way to integrate your goals into your lifestyle, not compete with it.

Having a perfect game plan to make something happen for you is also not enough. The formula could be right in front of you, a step-by-step plan on how to guarantee success for yourself, by it still doesn't work out. Why? Adherence.

Adherence is the quality of devotion, allegiance, attachment, or sticking to something. If we are talking lifestyle goals and rules, it is your ability to stick to the plan, to have staying power and determination.

Why do you think so many diets fail, and people who go on them end up returning to their starting weight? Why do so many new year's resolutions never come to pass? Why do people drop out of courses? It's not always because the actual diet doesn't work, or the goal is impossible, or the course doesn't teach you what it claims to. It is because people, in general, have poor adherence rates.

Humans are complex. We are made up of patterns of behaviour, ingrained beliefs about ourselves and the world, habits, and our knowledge of ourselves and things around us. Remember how I mentioned the concept of a schema at the start of this book, and how it represents a pattern of thinking that each individual has to help them interpret the world? Each individual, depending on their upbringing, the lessons they have learned, and their life experiences, will have their own unique schemas, which will help them or hinder them in different areas. Though we can change our schemas, being aware of these differences is key to setting productive goals for ourselves.

There are so many variables from person to person that no two people experience achieving a goal in the same way. What is easy for one person seems near impossible for the other and vice versa. For example: Why are there so many different workout styles out there? One major reason is that people all have different ways of adhering to things. That is why when you start exercising, you may have to try several different modalities before you find something that works for you, that increases the likelihood that you will stick to a routine. And once you find a class, instructor, program, or exercise style you love, it becomes much easier to do it regularly.

In 2021, a meta-analysis by Daniel Collado-Mateo et al. discussed key factors that were associated with adherence to physical exercise, and found a large range of factors (fourteen) that contributed.[1] One was enjoyment of the task, meaning that if something was too painful or the recovery took too long, people were less likely to continue. Another factor was having slightly lower expectations versus higher, because doing well made their long-term goals feel more achievable for them, and therefore more motivating to see them through. Supervision was also a big factor, which is probably why people pay a personal trainer to get them to do a workout they might be able to do alone: it increases their chances of following through. And another huge factor here was self-efficacy, which is the person's belief in being able to carry out a task.

Self-efficacy is another concept that's closely tied to adherence, and I want to give you a better sense of exactly what it is and how it can help you.

Psychologist Albert Bandura, the person responsible for creating the theoretical construct of self-efficacy, speaks to this in his book *Self-Efficacy: The Exercise of Control*. Self-efficacy refers to an individual's belief in their capacity to execute behaviours necessary to produce specific performance attainments. Basically, it's your belief in your own self as far as your abilities are concerned; your belief in your ability to achieve something, to heal from something physical or emotional, to bounce back from defeat, your ability to grow, etc. And it is involved in every area of human behaviour. What you believe is possible for you to achieve or attain bleeds into all areas of achievement in your life, whether it be career, relationships, experiences, wealth, health, or knowledge.

Whatever your level of self-efficacy is will determine how you think and behave. Those behaviours then influence future beliefs about yourself, ultimately creating a positive feedforward loop. And this determines whether you will stick something out or not: adherence.

If you set a goal and fail, it doesn't necessarily matter in the long run. Remember what we learned about working towards a growth mindset: true success is more about your willingness to give it a go and see what sticks. If your self-efficacy is low, you look for reasons why you can't do something, or what might make it difficult for you to do it. You might think, *I'm not as smart as my peers, so I won't apply for that job; the market is saturated, so I won't launch this product or business or podcast; I am not confident in social settings, so I won't try to meet new friends.*

Why is this internal belief so important? Because it is what will determine what kind of goals you set for yourself, and the calibre and size of these goals. It will also determine *how* you will go after these goals: whether you approach them with one foot in the door and one out or if you're 100 per cent all-in, if you will throw minimal resources at it versus risking more. It all comes down to self-efficacy.

If you think something's impossible to achieve, then the likelihood of you sticking to it is going to be low. You will have an emotional aversion to it before you even begin. And when you embark on a challenge, not considering how likely you are to stick to it can be detrimental for the next time you set out to achieve a goal.

No matter what it is you're looking to accomplish, I really want you to start creating a standard of sticking it out with something. If you fail to achieve a goal because it is too unbearable to stick to the plan, it leaves you feeling worse off, defeated, and less likely to be able to throw yourself all-in on your next attempt at something. Remember we talked about the stories we attach ourselves to in module one? By doing this, you're creating a narrative of yourself as a quitter, and you might regularly find yourself back where you started, struggling to make progress.

To create a true lifestyle change for yourself, something that becomes a part of you long term, it's important to not be so rigid when it comes to timelines to achieving your goal; this is where so many people go wrong. Understand that by considering adherence and self-efficacy when you set your goals, your progress may be slower, but the payoff is that the results are lasting. Your lifestyle improves.

So let's look at ways you can start to break down these barriers to entry and edit how you go about achieving your goal. Let's begin with reasons that you may have used when you quit something in the past, and ways you can work around them.

1. 'It's too hard.' If a goal simply feels too hard to achieve, find ways of surrounding yourself with people at a similar level or reducing the intensity or workload so it becomes achievable. Remember: you actually *save* time this way. By pushing your timeline further out, you'll only have to do it once, rather than quitting and starting the same process twenty times.
2. 'I'm too bored.' Again, you may need to find ways of creating community around what you do. Take exercise, for example: you can join a walking or running club or do a group class where you are told what to do and don't have to go through it alone. If your goal has to do with food, make sure you are creating a balanced meal plan with lot of options, so you have variety.

3. 'I'm embarrassed.' Seek out others who have done what you want to do, in person or through research or interviews, and expand your awareness of how people have started where you are starting. Find a mentor who can make you feel comfortable about where you are in your journey – even if this mentor is just someone you look up to online and have never met.

Remember: The best plan is the one you stick to. Does it matter if it is perfect? No – not if 'imperfect' means you are more likely to see something through to the end. What is the point of having a strict, regimented lifestyle goal if you can never stick to it, and, when you try to, it makes you absolutely miserable in the process? There is no point. Because it only increases the likelihood of you dropping out and negatively impacting your self-efficacy.

So make sure you are not wasting time forcing yourself to stick to something that simply does not work for you. Instead, shop around for things that fit, things that work for you as much as you work for them. Try things out for size until you are satisfied; many of the daily tasks in this book are designed to help you do just that. Just because something worked for your best friend does not mean it will work for you, so it is important you take an approach of tailoring your lifestyle to yourself, and not the other way around.

Your daily task

As an exercise, take a look at a goal of yours, ideally one you have tried before and not succeeded at, and pull apart what you did and didn't do the last time around. So often, people set a goal, fail at it, and then set the same goal again without changing how they plan to go about it. If the plan was flawed the first time, what makes you think it will go great this time? It's not that you cannot achieve your goals, it's that you need to look at what went wrong and change the pathway to the outcome. And you can change that today. Call out what went wrong and why and decide what needs to change to increase the likelihood of you adhering to the plan.

An example I can give is that I always wanted to exercise regularly. For years, I would train in the afternoon; I loved training in the afternoon, as it was a great way for me to wind down. However, I am also a very social person. On many afternoons, I would take an invitation to meet with a friend over the gym. What is the issue here? I have a social lifestyle, and I was not willing to give up that part of my life in order to stick to a new routine. I'm self-aware, and I've taken full accountability for not making this goal a reality in the past. So now, I have lost the privilege of training in the afternoon, and I switched to the mornings, a simple shift that made it so much easier for me to adhere to the plan. You have to identify what your lifestyle is, what you are willing to give up and what you are not, and then create goals that work for you as much as you work for them.

4.3 Name it to tame it: pushing past discomfort to stay on track.

In module two, we talked all about why we're wired to avoid discomfort. But by now, you understand that discomfort is a gift. It is an opportunity, a shake-up, a slap in the face. It is a second chance. And every time you are faced with pain or discomfort, you have a choice to either retreat or to grow. And when you are faced with discomfort every day, you are offered the potential to grow into your next phase.

And the reality is, shying away from discomfort does not eliminate it. It simply postpones the discomfort and magnifies it for later. The discomfort of doing that daily task is never as bad as the discomfort of looking back at your life and feeling as though you wasted your potential, knowing full well you had the skills and ability to accomplish your goals. If you go through life constantly trying to find ways to avoid discomfort, distracting yourself with pleasantries and searching for happiness in other areas, you begin to teach your brain how to approach this feeling. The more you avoid it, the more the brain believes that it's something to be feared, so it sets itself up to avoid it at all costs to protect you from pain.

And this happens to us in small ways all the time; when you feel your mood shift negatively, you might initially seek to distract or run away from the problem. This does not actually make the feeling go away but leads to a tendency to rely on distracting behaviours to get by. This is why endlessly scrolling on your phone or engaging in distracting tasks can be such a difficult habit to break. Not only is the act itself distracting and addictive, but it stops you from having to face these uncomfortable thoughts and feelings.

My goal is to help you become the best version of yourself, but that does *not* mean every moment is going to be beautiful and every thought will be a happy one. Every moment will not be perfect, positive, and happy. How can it be? And if you fall into the trap of thinking that a successful life is one that is void of uncomfortable and painful moments, then you will always feel like you are 'not there yet' or that there is something wrong with how your mind operates, which is not the case. Instead of feeling like your brain is working against you, you have to realise that it's simply doing what it has been conditioned to do. And if it has always known to avoid discomfort, it is going to do anything it possibly can to get you to avoid it in the future. When you train your brain to do the opposite, soon enough your brain will feel like it is on your side.

Embracing and facing discomfort is a huge power move. You stop being a victim to your circumstances, and you take the wheel. For me, it is one of the best forms of self-love. It is treating the future me as a priority and doing something to help her.

Now, let's talk about how we tackle uncomfortable emotions so they don't keep growing and taking over.

The first problem is that often we don't even know what caused our anxiety in the first place. So maybe you let it grow in the background and can't work out why you feel different, as if there is a weight on you. One of the best things to do is to stop everything you are doing and ask yourself, *When was this shift? When did I start feeling differently?* Try to *pinpoint* that moment. In most cases, if you really focus, you will be able to.

This technique, first coined by psychiatrist Dr Daniel Siegel, is called 'name it to tame it'.[1] Sometimes, you let your thoughts run wild and end up thinking an issue is bigger than what you can handle. But the moment you clearly address it, you can see you have control, and that thing is no longer controlling you. Maybe you'll remember it was an email that set you off, or the fact that the person you like didn't reply to your message straight away, and you started thinking the worst. Or maybe the video you uploaded did not receive many likes, which caused you to doubt yourself, and in the back of your mind, you began to spiral without even realising it, until you started to feel intense physical symptoms like heart palpitations.

The moment you identify and name the cause, you can identify the mood shift. You were feeling fine this morning, and something has happened in between then and now, and now you feel low and anxious. Once you recognise that feeling, it immediately loses power over you. The simple act of naming it gives you back the control. It not only helps you deal with the emotions in the moment, but it trains your brain to gain control over big emotions as they come up in the future, instead of first spiralling and catastrophising your thoughts.

In a study at UCLA, Dr Michelle Craske tested this concept around labelling emotions with a group of participants that had a fear of spiders.[2] She made the participants get close to, and in some cases even touch, a large tarantula… I know, good times. Then she split the groups into four categories based on how they spoke about their fear.

One group straight-up named what was happening, saying things like, 'I am scared of this huge spider.' Another group said things they thought would make them less scared such as, 'This spider can't hurt me, it is in a cage!' The other group said something completely irrelevant to spiders to distract themselves, and the last group said nothing at all.

The team tracked physiological measurements, such as palm sweating and other physical responses, in the participants, and when all the groups were tested a week later with the same exercise, the first group (the one that named their fear) outperformed all the other groups based on how distressed they felt versus the first time.

Why is this so effective? The idea is that *naming* an emotion bridges the gap between logical thought and emotion. When we are feeling heightened emotions, we're being controlled by a part of the brain called the limbic system: the older, more primitive part of the brain consisting of components like the hippocampus and amygdala. The limbic system is responsible for our flight, fright, or freeze responses. When that area is activated, it's going to intensify the experience of an emotion, and make it feel all-encompassing.[3]

On the other hand, the prefrontal cortex of the brain is responsible for executive function, impulse control, and reasoning, and this is the part of the brain that does the naming, when you 'name it to tame it'. When the prefrontal cortex becomes reignited during a highly emotional moment, it kicks into reasoning and problem-solving mode, and counteracts the intensity of the activity happening within the reactive and emotional limbic system. This technique alone, regardless of what's happening with the spider or other cause for anxiety, begins to calm down the nervous system, because the regions of our brain begin to communicate in a more productive way. Interestingly, a similar thing happens during meditation, because the act of meditating helps increase connectivity between these brain regions.

The more you do this, the faster you will get your reasoning and logic to kick in, and soon your spiralling thoughts will dissipate. You will become more skilled at identifying what the source of your anxiety or fear is. And because you can identify it so fast, it won't get magnified into this insurmountable feeling where you are not motivated to do anything and find yourself seeking constant distraction. This one small change can permanently flip your perspective on discomfort.

Remember: you have more power than you think, even when you feel like your emotions or fears are spiralling out of control. Pinpoint your discomfort, and recognise it as the opportunity it can be. This will help you stay focused, disciplined, and on track in the face of hardship.

Your daily task

The next time these uncomfortable emotions creep up, I want you to practise the 'name it to tame it' method. Once you name that thing that's causing you discomfort, you can start to ask yourself the following questions:

1. When did this feeling of anxiety begin, and what was the initial cause or trigger?
2. Do I have power or control over this situation?
3. Am I catastrophising or generalising, and making the problem bigger than it really is? And am I able to narrow it down and get more specific about what's bothering me? (P.S. There are plenty of examples of this in our 'pain versus suffering' chapter, where we talked about inevitability of pain versus the choice to lean into suffering.)
4. What is the worst-case scenario right now?
5. On a scale of one to ten, what is the likelihood of the worst-case scenario happening?
6. Can I do something right now that will alleviate it? Pay the bill, reply to the message? Or is this something I truly cannot control?

> Doing this task even for the smallest emotions will train your mind to snap into action faster and faster. So now you no longer need to ignore these emotions; you can do something with them. Journal about it, write it down, talk it through with someone you trust; anything that helps you put your thoughts and feelings out of your emotional head and into a logical space will help you feel more in control.

4.4 Small time management changes that lead to life-altering habits.

Many people have this idea that in order to create change, the actions need to be drastic, and that is the only way. That's why when they're looking to discover their passion or achieve a goal, they get caught up in the label; they worry that if they settle on something they perceive to be small or basic, it will not satisfy them. So they keep searching for this mystical answer in a huge lifestyle change.

As you may have already noticed – not just in this book, but in many other teachings in self-development – progress, success, and fulfilment really come from smaller habits and behaviours. So if you think something's boring, easy, and mundane, but it could improve your day in some small way, maybe that is your cue to give it a go. There is nothing exciting about announcing a new ten-minute habit in your morning every day. And that is why you should do it anyway.

You also might hear people say that your goals should excite you. And this is true, but with conditions. I don't want you to think this means that each goal you set out to do should be filled with passion and enjoyment, and that if it is not enjoyable every day, it is not right. You should love your life, but you should also be prepared to do boring and mundane things in order to maintain the life you love. Avoiding boring tasks is a sure way of getting let down by your own goals. Don't feel as if they're not right for you because they are not enjoyable, or because you're not bouncing out of bed to do these tasks every day.

You do not have to love everything you do. There are many things you will have to do on a daily basis that you will not love, or even like. But it is the result that you love, it's the lifestyle that it gives you that you love: the health, longevity, the savings, the results, the opportunity that certain behaviours will afford you. The behaviours themselves are not all going to be great and fun-filled.

If something is a challenge in the short term, it will become easier for you in the long term with consistency. This can be applied to almost anything. Waking up early? Not fun in the first one to two minutes of getting out of bed, but it affords you time before work to do things for yourself. It beats getting up at the last minute and having all your attention and time eaten up by work or attending to tasks or people outside of yourself.

Going to exercise may not be fun in the moment, but the elevated energy levels and reduced stress throughout the day are definitely worth it. Cleaning the kitchen before bedtime even when you are exhausted is a drag, but waking up to a clean and organised home, where your mind feels calm and happier, is worth ten times more than the short-lived pleasure of putting off an inevitable task. Fun fact: Did you know that a messy living space can actually impact your brain? A 2010 study by two researchers at UCLA showed that participants who described their homes as cluttered were more likely to experience stress and depressed moods.[1]

Like we spoke about earlier in the identity module, your identity is ever-changing, and you have the opportunity to return to a clean canvas anytime. You can create a new habit or lifestyle and make that part of you, even if it seems so far-fetched. But as I have mentioned before, it has to be something that resonates with you, so you are most likely to adhere to it, and you need to see the benefits it provides.

So let's cover some simple strategies you can employ in your day-to-day that will help you work towards the big changes you want to see.

Delayed gratification and creating a simple rewards system

If I had a dollar for every time my mother yelled 'Delayed gratification!' at me, I'd be rich. When we were younger, she would always set tasks for my sister and me to do over the weekends, and we hated them. We used to whine for hours about having to sweep the entire backyard, but there would always be some sort of incentive, such as ice cream or some fun activity, although only if we had completed that task. And at the time, we thought she really needed us to be doing these tasks, but in hindsight, I think she was just trying to instil a very valuable lesson that we both still use daily.

We learned that you could get a lot more done, and faster, if there was something gratifying at the end. And I also learned that if I did have something nice to enjoy, such as watching an episode of my favourite TV show, drinking a coffee, eating something I love, relaxing to read a chapter of a book, or going out for dinner with friends, I could tackle a few boring tasks *beforehand*, and that would become my version of delayed gratification. Now I know even the smallest task will be done as long as I have a reward in mind. For example, I'll unload the dishwasher before a coffee, or fold a few pieces of clothes before getting dressed and ready to go out, or make my bed before going to meet a friend for a walk.

If you, like so many of us, love scrolling on social media, then you can really use this to your advantage. Try doing three small house chores or forty minutes of housework to earn ten minutes of scrolling on your phone, and it no longer feels like you are wasting your time away. It works every time, and even on the days where you feel super demotivated to get anything done, it will get you knocking over *something* on your to-do list, even just a tiny task.

If you are stuck for ideas on the right rewards, write a long list of possible small, medium, and large rewards for yourself. The small ones are like the ones I just mentioned: enjoyable things that you would normally already do day-to-day. Medium rewards are great for when you complete a larger task. This could be an essay, project, a job application – anything that represents completing a larger job that isn't part of your daily routine. And for large rewards, where you may be spending a sum of money on yourself, I like to reserve these for big accomplishments, such as completing a course or hitting a career milestone. These could also work for having implemented lasting change for more than six months, such as a morning routine, or quitting smoking, etc. Have a hierarchy of rewards that are proportionate to your goals. These small and large incentives are a great way to remind yourself of what is around the corner. Which leads me to my next point:

Timed tasks and time blocking

Not every task can be completed in one sitting. Think of practising for something, writing an essay or book, studying for something, or putting together a pitch for work. So much goes into any of these things! And on the flip side, there are tasks that are so small that only doing one doesn't feel like you have accomplished much, such as responding to an email or putting away a few things around the house. This is where timed tasks and time blocking will transform your productivity and get you knocking over a lot of work on a regular basis.

Often you may wait until you have an entire weekend off, or a half day to yourself, to dedicate to a large task before you begin. But these opportunities are few and far between, and they also don't help you create consistency, as they do not come up often. Instead of having a goal to finish something, dedicate a time-based goal: a certain amount of time you're committing to that activity, no matter how big or small a dent you can make on the big-picture task. Once that time is done, you are done for the day, and then you move onto the next thing.

This helps you create a realistic expectation, and it reduces distractions, as you are not switching from task to task, breaking focus each time. You only have to get into the zone for the task once; you're not repeatedly trying to get your focus back. Instead of replying to emails and texts as they come in, set a twenty-minute time between tasks to knock them over, and do that two or three times in a day, rather than checking your emails thirty times a day, each time a new one rolls in.

The truth is, almost no one can properly multitask. It reduces productivity and also compromises your quality of work. Ever noticed how difficult it is to return to a task after spending a few minutes on your phone? The goal here is to focus on one task at a time for that time block, say, forty-five minutes to an hour, before shifting your focus to the next job.

For those who swear multitasking works for them, I'll add that the neuroscientific evidence around it doesn't sound promising. A study by Madore and Wagner showed that the brain struggles to perform two tasks simultaneously, which therefore impacts your ability to perform even a basic task. Their 2019 article, 'Multicosts of Multitasking', argues that the term itself is inaccurate.[2] The brain isn't set up to tackle two tasks simultaneously; what it's actually doing is switching back and forth between the tasks rapidly. So, if you feel that your whole day is being wasted away and you didn't get much done, take a look at your time management and how you split tasks. You may be doing yourself a disservice. Limit distraction, focus on one task at a time, and do it regularly. And by putting the focus on time spent and not needing to complete the task at hand, you remove the stress and pressure that goes with it, and just do what you can do in that hour.

One of the biggest disservices you can do yourself on this journey is expecting to love every single aspect of your day. That is what procrastinators do, and that is what happens when you choose instant gratification over delayed gratification. You can't always be choosing the enjoyable over the important. This is what will keep you living in your potential, unrealised, waiting for that big idea or big inspiration to come and slap you in the face. All the while, time is passing by.

And that moment never comes because this is within *your* control. *You* must find it; it does not find you. And you find it though action, effort, trial and error, and chipping away small amounts each day until you carve out something for yourself that you can be proud of, that can become your passion. And that journey does not have to be glamorous – it just has to be done consistently.

Your daily task

I want you to start implementing time blocking into your week.

To begin, write a list of tasks that you need to get done tomorrow, and categorise them as urgent (but truly urgent, be strict here), important (the tasks that will really make you feel fulfilled and satisfied, or contribute to your health, such as exercise and meditation), or optional (something that you'd like to get done, but don't absolutely need to). Then identify if the task is ongoing (hours spent towards work, or an essay that will take a few days) or one-off (booking your car in for a service).

Now, choose the time duration for each time block. I love to do forty-five minutes of work and a fifteen-minute break to give my mind a rest from focused activity. When I write a list of what I want done, I make sure that I put the tasks that require the most attention or focus (the more cognitively difficult tasks) at the top of the list and the easier tasks further down. As the day goes on, you do not want to leave the hard tasks to the end, as that is when fatigue and decision fatigue set in, and it is harder to maintain focus or make decisions quickly.

I try to allocate four time blocks to my day, and if I can do more, it feels like a bonus. I'd encourage you to start with two lots of time blocks and increase from there.

When time blocking, there are three aims. First, to learn to tackle one task at a time and eliminate distractions for the allocated time slot (goodbye multitasking). Second, to learn to increase your focus and attention span, and therefore achieve more in less time. Third, to tackle something from each of the categories listed so you feel more balanced at the end of the day, knowing you have done something to satisfy at least something in each area. Without time blocking, you may never get there, because you have not prioritised your tasks in the way you want.

4.5 How to harness dopamine and make it work for you, not against you.

We are currently living in an era of a serious attention problem. So many of the things we use on a daily basis are designed to grab our attention. And unless you are acutely aware of how this happens, it will be difficult to learn how to control it, and you will fall prey to it constantly, wasting a lot of time in the process.

If you want real control over your life, you're going to have to know how to harness dopamine so you can maximise your focus and attention. Because without being able to guide your own attention and control your impulses, you are not really in the driver's seat. You will be a victim to distractions, spiralling thoughts, addictive behaviours, and not get much of the important stuff done. If you are struggling with focus and even feel like there may be something wrong with you, then read on, because you have more control than you realise.

I love watching adults who are so fascinated with babies and toddlers when they gravitate to phones. Every time this happens, I hear a comment along the lines of, 'Can you believe it! They just go straight for the phone! Look at how they are magnetised to it!' Parents will talk about how difficult it is to get their children not to use devices once they have discovered them, and how hooked they become to playing games on an iPad. All this is true, but I find it funny, because we adults are really no better. The only actual difference is that when the device is removed from an adult, we do not have a visible public tantrum or meltdown, and that's just because we have the advantage of having the emotional maturity to regulate our emotions in public. However, our impulse control when it comes to using devices is extremely low, sometimes as low as young children. We will subconsciously reach for our devices only moments after putting them away, or circle back to the same app we just closed a few seconds ago in hopes of finding something new and exciting that will spike our interest. So next time you see a child with a phone or device, remind yourself that adults, for the most part, are not much better, and this is something that you should want to change for yourself.

I am all for using devices, how could I not be? They are pivotal for my job and have allowed me to reach an audience and do well in my career. But just like the mind, you want to learn to *use* technology, and not let it use you. My aim for you is to have all these tools at your disposal to *help* you create the life you want to experience, and never feel hostage to them. And I don't want you thinking you have to go cold turkey, either. Balance in pretty much everything is what I try to aim for – not perfection. And with a little bit of tweaking your behaviours, balance is definitely achievable here.

Let's first talk dopamine, because this neurotransmitter has the ability to control you and drive you. It is the chemical responsible for impulse control, or lack thereof. Dopamine is commonly known as the 'rewards' neurotransmitter.[1] It is heavily involved in behavioural and chemical addictions, and is responsible for your willingness to do things. It is what gets you repeating that behaviour, whether you're smoking a cigarette or reaching for your phone for the twentieth time this hour.

But no neurotransmitter should be labelled good or bad. They are all useful for their intended purpose. There is a reason for each chemical existing, and when put to use properly, they help the brain maintain homeostasis, and help the person have a happy and meaningful life. It is your job to understand and then to harness the power in them.

The problem with dopamine is that it can be depleted pretty easily. And if you are always reaching for quick hits like checking notifications, receiving likes, receiving hits of validation for little to no effort, then you're getting all these little spikes of dopamine. While it is not as aggressive as a chemical drug addiction, the brain does respond in a similar way. Every time it spikes and goes up, it must come down, and this is where it drops below baseline before it can return to its normal level, which takes some time. The more of these spikes you get, the more you deplete your levels of dopamine, and it becomes harder and harder to return to baseline. And because dopamine is the motivation chemical, it is no wonder you feel like it's so difficult to hold focus on a task that either requires more effort or that is mundane. Your brain is not only drawn to an addictive behaviour to get that spike, but at the same time it struggles to do other tasks.

That is why if you spend an hour or even thirty minutes on your phone, it feels near impossible to feel motivated to do anything else that requires even the slightest effort. Once the dopamine is depleted, the effort it takes to get off the couch and do that task seems insurmountable. It's not about what you are physically capable of doing, it's whether or not your brain has enough motivation to get you up to tackle that task.

This is why you end up procrastinating and feeling flat. Then, of course, in order to feel better, what do you do? Reach for the phone, device, cigarette, or any quick hit of dopamine to make you feel good again. Sounds pretty similar to an addict's behaviour, doesn't it?

Now, again, dopamine isn't inherently bad, and there are many ways you can gently increase your levels of dopamine without having that high spike and a drop below baseline. This can be achieved through exercise, getting outside in the morning into sunlight, breath work, working on a task with meaning or purpose behind it, saunas, ice baths, and so much more. Even acts of kindness to others, including strangers, is a great way of boosting your levels of dopamine. When levels are elevated in this way, they can be sustained longer; you are then more likely to not only be driven to start a task but also to stay focused on that task, as elevated levels of dopamine increase attention, memory, and motivation.

The reason why exercise, morning sunlight, and meditation do not cause a drop of dopamine below baseline like phone usage or addictive behaviours comes down to a few things. Exercising or meditating requires a level of effort, self-control, and attention to do that task. The 'high' you feel is earned, and not passive. Not only is dopamine being released but so are endorphins, and the activities are helping regulate your cortisol release at the same time. Because it is a healthy increase in dopamine and not an instant gratification spike, you do not experience the sharp drop below baseline after exposure.

However, with addictive behaviours that require little to no effort to feel pleasure, the dopamine is not earned. The activity is extremely stimulating, and the rush of dopamine for these easy but distracting behaviours is faster and higher than what is produced doing something like exercising. It is not sustainable, and therefore dips lower than before you engaged in this instant gratification activity. If something gives you the kind of rush that seems to override other desires or causes you to procrastinate, chances are it is something that will make your dopamine dip below baseline and lower your motivation overall across the board. If the thing requires effort (for example, exercise) and does not make you drop everything to do more of the same, then it is a pretty safe bet that it is giving you a healthy, prolonged elevation in dopamine release. This will now make you more willing to do other things (motivation) instead of making you want to collapse and rot on the couch all afternoon.

Your attention should be looked at as a limited commodity, like money in your bank account or the days left in your life. Each day, you have a certain amount of focused attention to give. And if you waste it on things that do not serve you or better your state of mind, then you will be left with the dregs, the bottom of the barrel, the bare minimum. This is where you end up doing the minimum required tasks to be able to get by each day, just enough so you are not drowning in your responsibilities. And remember, every choice you make trains your brain how to behave, so the more you throw your attention to addictive behaviours, the shorter your attention span gets. You could end up living in this state of doing the bare minimum. A year can go by, and you wonder where your time went, but instead you should be asking, *Where did my attention go?* Focused attention will allow you to get more done in less time. And like I wrote about in the previous chapter, time blocking is a great way to begin to overcome issues with scattered attention.

I also want to encourage you to work with what you know. If you *know* you are going to be easily distracted, set yourself up in an environment where it's harder to reach your phone. Do not reattempt goals without first understanding what traps or bait tripped you up the first time. If you fell for it before, you will fall for it again. I sometimes will place my phone on the other side of the room when I need to concentrate. And even then, I notice my hand reach for my phone when it's not there. This snaps me out of it and gets me back on task. Had the phone been there, I would have been a robot on autopilot, scrolling for who knows how long. A lot of the time you don't even realise you picked up your device until after you unlocked it and have opened an app. Don't let these impulses control you. *You* are in control.

Your daily task

I want you to come up with ways that you can block yourself from using your phone impulsively. Some people delete certain apps at the start of the day and redownload them later; some have a way of locking themselves out of an app after using it too much. If this works for you, that's great, but personally, I find these too easy to get around, and find that the best way is the old-fashioned way of keeping it on the other side of the room when I don't need it. That is enough for me to snap out of a trance.

Today, try to limit phone use during your times of highest focus, which are different for us all. If your mornings are for performing high-focus tasks, leave the social media for the afternoons so you can dedicate all your high-attention 'quota' for the day to the important tasks. Addictive behaviours should never replace important tasks. They are never worth it, and they will leave you feeling like you wasted something you will never get back. Try this today and remind yourself of this each morning to help you prioritise your time.

4.6 Let your results speak for themselves.

Do you feel that sharing your goals with others will make you accountable and more likely to follow through? A lot of people do, and they use this as a tool when they want to embark on a challenge. However, I want you to be honest about how often this has *actually* worked for you. Do you really find this method helpful? If not, there are ways you can improve it so you are more likely to follow through.

Psychologist Peter Gollwitzer published a study focused around goal sharing and motivation, and the result may surprise you.[1] Gollwitzer and his colleagues found that people who spoke about their goals to others were actually *less* likely to follow through, because they felt a sense of accomplishment before having achieved it.

People get super-excited to run a marathon, change their lifestyle, start a new hobby, or launch their new business, and often they tell everyone they know. Of course, they then receive all these accolades for their intention to do something. People say, 'Wow, how impressive!' or 'I'm so excited for you.' Then there is less drive or motivation to actually do that thing, because you have already received the praise.

You create a goal partly because you want to feel great for having achieved it. And that sense of achievement can come from within, but who doesn't like to be praised by those around them? The moment the goal has been shared, you already experience part of that feeling, part of that reward. But receiving the reward before you have started the work wastes the effect of that feeling before you have begun. It is like letting yourself eat that ice cream before you have cleaned the house (if you have taken on my tip of delayed gratification). Now there's not much left to motivate you to clean the house.

Imagine if you could never again tell people what you were going to do, and the only way of letting them know was to show them through your actions. Would anything change in how you approach your goals? Would you be more driven to spend time on the task? Would you be more excited to start seeing results, instead of just talking about them?

When I saw what these studies showed, it struck a chord with me, because I used to be a massive over-sharer of what I wanted to do with my life. I would often share these big decisions prematurely, well before I had even fleshed out the plan of attack in my own head. And the problem for me was that often, not long after sharing, I would either decide it wasn't for me, that I needed to alter the vision, or I just wasn't as excited as I had initially thought. Then I would start to feel like my word didn't carry much weight. I wanted to be a person who did what I said I would do, not someone who's all talk. So, hearing about these studies really got me excited to try a different approach.

It helped me become a person of my word, because from then on, I would only speak about a new goal when I had already put things in motion. This also gave me the opportunity to sit with the idea, think it over on my own, and see if it was just excitement in the moment, a flash in the pan that I would get over, or if it really was something that I had tenacity for.

That saying 'Don't make promises when you are happy' really applied to me, because I would get so happy and excited about these different ideas. But once the initial euphoria wore off, I realised certain things had less weight than I initially thought. And in learning to hold some things back, I learned a lot about myself, what I really want, and what I am truly willing to work for versus what sounds nice to talk about.

Now, when I really want something for myself, I limit the people who know. The more I want to do something, the more it matters to me, the smaller the circle I tell. And when something is *really* important to me, I tell no one at all through my words. I say to myself, 'If I am serious enough, I will be able to tell people about it, but only through my actions. They will find out about it by observing.' And because I am a sharer at heart and always want to discuss what I'm doing with those close to me, this fuels me and hurries me along to act, because without action, I cannot share anything.

This technique has made me get up off my ass and start many things, including my podcast. I only told people about it *after* I bought a microphone, recorded the first episode, and was ready to upload it. The idea for the podcast came to me less than two months before launching, after I was a guest on my friend's podcast. I loved everything about that experience. Plus, I had banged on about starting a YouTube channel for a long time and had never done it – so I wanted to approach this idea differently, by truly going for it *before* sharing the goal. I finally had something I could talk endlessly about: all the fascinating information I was learning as I worked towards my master's degree, which I couldn't shut up about. So this was the perfect incentive for me to start right away. I couldn't wait to share it with everyone, but until it was ready, I kept my mouth shut to most people I knew.

Less than a week before I launched my podcast, I spoke to my cousin to brainstorm a name. I liked the word 'mind' or 'mindset', and we kept throwing ideas around until Lorena said, 'Do You F*cking Mind?' I thought, *That is it. I will not overthink it; it sounds right, so it is right.* I committed to it, and the next day I made the artwork on a free app and recorded the episode. The following day, it was live. When you have a fire inside you to share what you are excited to do, you will be amazed at how efficiently you will move on that project.

Of course, telling relevant people who can help you along the way to a certain goal can be great – like I did with my cousin. Another example may be if your friend is embarking on the same journey, or if someone can mentor you or give you sound advice, or if you live together and your lifestyle is going to change as a result of this new goal. These are all fine and should not hinder your progress. I just don't want you to fall into the trap of relying on others to motivate you. You will be amazed at how driven you will become when you restrict yourself to expressing what you are doing through actions alone. That's when you know how serious you are. If you cannot do it that way, then maybe you are not that serious about this particular goal.

How many times have we all been in a situation where we are so pumped to do something that we tell everyone we meet, under the impression that this will make us more accountable? As I mentioned earlier in this book, the ultimate accountability buddy is yourself. People all have their own stuff going on, so even if you do share it in your group text or to your social media following, who is *really* going to be following up, making sure you are hitting these goals? Not many, if any. And at times, believing that others will help keep us accountable can actually be a hinderance, because we end up relying on them too much for motivation, for inspiration. If you're waiting for them to go first and to help keep you in line, you run the risk of becoming complacent.

When we tell people about how our entire life will change, they get excited in the moment on our behalf, and we feel a rush, a sense of accomplishment. Then we get home. The excitement is wearing off, and we think, *I'll start tomorrow*. Then tomorrow rolls around, only for us to not feel anywhere near as excited, because we have already been celebrating something before the work has been done. And we realise how little telling someone about something makes us stay accountable. Part of achieving something is being able to see the results and share them. But if you give yourself the prize before the work, then a big chunk of those incentives could be diminished or taken away.

Now, if you are hellbent on telling people your goals, there is a way to go about it. In the examples I've shared so far, by telling people early, you lose nothing by not following through. There are no direct consequences for your lack of action. So if you are going to share with others, there *must* be a penalty or consequence. And it is better to be driven by a penalty than by a reward, because, as you now know, we value the prospect of losing something more than we value the prospect of gaining. As we learned in module two, loss looms larger than gains. The studies we discussed in module two demonstrated that people place greater value on an item they have to give up versus one they may acquire.

So what will it be? A financial penalty? A favour that you have to follow through with? If the penalty seems too harsh and you don't want to do that, then it is a clear indication that maybe you should keep this goal to yourself until you are sure you can pull it off.

Your daily task

I want you to think of a goal that you hold close to your heart, something that really matters to you, no matter how embarrassing or how outrageous or how selfish you think it sounds. Maybe it's something you've already documented in another daily-task exercise. Get clear on what achieving that goal would look like. Is it practising a language for thirty minutes a day? Is it applying for a course you hope to get into? Starting your own channel or podcast?

Now, pick a milestone that you must achieve *before* you tell anyone, like I did by buying equipment and recording my first podcast episode. Make sure that milestone requires some serious effort, not just brainstorming and planning. This could be signing up for a course and paying a deposit; it could be creating the first five steps of your business plan, something that demonstrates skin in the game. Then commit to yourself. Make this one promise today: until that milestone is hit, it is your own little secret. You will find that relying on yourself is exciting, and it actually becomes *more* exciting knowing you did this all on your own. Start today.

4.7 The truth about discipline and freedom.

What do you consider freedom to be? When you think of someone who is very disciplined, you may think of someone who has a very regimented life, without many freedoms or opportunities to be spontaneous. And for a lot of us, that sounds like a pretty boring, unappealing lifestyle. Is freedom, for you, the ability to get up and do whatever you want? To go where the wind takes you on a daily basis? Or is it having resources to access the experiences and health (both mental and physical) that you want? I want you to think about this deeply, because what may appear to be freedom at face value can actually cause you to feel very restricted later on in life.

Let me explain: there are going to be things that are detrimental to your health in the short term that *feel* like freedom right now. Let's take spending money as an example. In this case, living too much 'for the now', spending whatever you wish, and not taking care of what you have so you can put it to use in the future will ultimately leave you very restricted years down the line. It will have a negative impact on your overall freedom.

So, in essence, there are two kinds of freedom: one where it's all about right here, right now, and your future self suffers, and one that requires discipline, where you will set yourself up to continuously reap the benefits. It is up to you to decide what kind of freedom you are looking for in this life, because you can't have both. And are you really free if you do not have your health or the resources you need to support yourself?

We all love the sound of freedom, but the truth is, the brain loves discipline and structure. They allow it to feel comfortable, and give it a sense of clarity and purpose. They allow your brain to automate simple tasks, so it can free up effort to focus on new or more challenging ones. When there is routine and structure, your mind is calmer and happier, and only then does it allow for the kind of freedom of thought where creativity can thrive. You need that sense of control over yourself to truly be free.

Take Steve Jobs, for example. He famously wore the same outfit every day, a black turtleneck with jeans and sneakers, so there was one less decision he had to make.[1] This helped hold off the decision-making fatigue that sets in for everyone after too many choices need to be made. A lot of successful people are seen wearing the same or similar outfits on repeat to save time and effort, so they can invest that time in other things.

Personally, I change up my outfits, but I relate to this line of thinking in other ways: I never have to think about when I am going to meditate, as I do it every morning immediately after waking up. My alarm goes off, I drink a large glass of water by my bed, I meditate for ten minutes, and then I get dressed to exercise. Doing this has not only ensured I meditate regularly, but it has saved me contemplating, procrastinating, and going back and forth figuring out when in the day I can squeeze in a meditation. Outsource these tasks to your subconscious mind by making them repetitive, and then you never have to make that decision again. It is done.

I want you to start looking at freedom in a brand-new way. Discipline and freedom are two closely intertwined things; you cannot have one without the other, as counterintuitive as it seems. To really understand this, consider this question: If you could have more freedom, what would that look like? For a child, it would probably be eating whatever they want and staying up all night. But for you, an adult, what would freedom be? Being able to say no more often? Being able to have more alone time? Being able to purchase things? Travel more? Have physical health? Feel happier and calmer?

With all those things mentioned under the 'adult freedom' category, *discipline* is what can get you there. Discipline is your ticket to the life you want to have. It will give you opportunities; it will give you independence, income, time, and a balanced life. If you do not have discipline, you are not going to have access to all these things. You can also look at it this way: discipline gives you the options you would have never had otherwise. With more freedom comes more choice, more control over where you steer your life, and, therefore, more opportunities and experiences.

So try not to think of discipline as being too regimented, or all about structure and restricting spontaneity. Discipline actually *allows* for spontaneity. It gives you access. The resources that discipline affords are endless.

For years, I craved exactly this sense of in-the-moment freedom in my life, like the child who thinks being free means having no bedtime. I thought that I didn't like being tied down, and the thought of settling in one location for too long freaked me out, because I thought it would hold me back. I thought that laying down roots was the equivalent to having my wings clipped. I would look at people my age buying their own home and starting a family and feel like that was the most restrictive thing. I even avoided purchasing furniture for the longest time, because it was too much of an indicator that I was grounded in one spot.

But every time I travelled, this lack of structure was what kept me having to return back home to scramble to get more money.

Then I would take off again, restarting the cycle. I was never able to really build anything for myself, because I was always chasing this feeling of freedom. During this time, I was blocking my ability to really experience freedom, because I had no staying power in anything. I wasn't sticking it out, and I wasn't saving money the way I could have, because it didn't fit into my narrative of not wanting to be tied down. This ironically made me *more* tied down, not to a location but to my own limitations. There was a limit to what I could afford, experience, and achieve, and there always would be if I never committed to seeing something through long term. It wasn't until I gave in to my desire of returning to study neuroscience that I was forced to stop, be in one location, and settle into that lifestyle that I discovered how much untapped potential I had been sitting on.

The years in my life where I had the least amount of freedom were those when I had the least amount of discipline. As I returned to Australia to study my master's, work a consistent job, and create an exercise routine, the more disciplined I became, and, for the first time, I began to really build something. I never realised how important this linear progression of cumulative work would be to my life. Instead of doing clumps of work here and there, I was able to focus on something and watch it continue to grow. I could build on ideas, concepts, knowledge, and creativity. This provided me with more resources, time, and money, which I could use to provide myself with the freedoms that I craved so much in the past. For me, that was travelling. What I thought would be the biggest cock block to my life of freedom actually provided me everything I wanted. And it all came from a disciplined, habitual lifestyle. I was finally able to do something in my spare time aside from work and sleep. And I had to admit, being disciplined and laying some roots down was a wonderful thing. I loved everything about it, and I never lost anything that I had feared losing. I only gained.

Discipline falls into many categories, a lot of which we've discussed in this book: the discipline of sticking to habits and routines, the discipline of choosing delayed gratification over instant gratification, and the discipline of making the hard decisions in the moment to help the you of the future, instead of leaving the tough stuff for later. Avoiding these hard decisions can keep you in jobs you hate, social dynamics where you are treated poorly, and it can keep you in really unhealthy relationships. And I would argue that the more disciplined you are, the more control you have over your mind and yourself, and the easier it is to remove yourself from what does not align with what is best for you overall.

Discipline improves your relationship with yourself and with others. It shows others how you treat yourself. And when people see you treat yourself with respect, they often follow suit. It is impossible to make someone feel worthless if they value themself. It may seem trivial that a simple daily structure can do this for you, but it is always the small daily habits that are responsible for big life changes. A big gesture once in a blue moon is not what will create lasting change. It is showing up for the small things again and again, day in and day out.

Your daily task

Have you ever heard of 'habit stacking'? It's the idea that you can incorporate a new task into your routine by stacking it on top of something you already do, and was popularised by James Clear in his bestselling book, *Atomic Habits.*[2] It's also a great way to get more disciplined and minimise decision fatigue by doing something on autopilot.

To start, write a list of tasks that you do every single day: things like silencing your alarm, brushing your teeth, taking your dog for a walk, etc. Now make another list of things you would like to do every day, but do not yet: examples of this might be meditating, exercising, reading ten pages a day, practising a language for fifteen minutes, journalling, flossing, taking vitamins, laying out your outfit for the following day, etc. Now, out of the tasks you have written down on the second list, how many of them can you bunch together with those on the first, the things you're already doing? If you can 'stack' two or more things together, then when one of these tasks is done, you automatically go onto the next task without distraction.

Instead of washing your face when you wake up, and then checking your phone, and then maybe getting dressed, wasting more time, then thirty minutes later finally leaving your home, you could be doing five small but important tasks back-to-back. That way, you cut out the time spent procrastinating or deciding what to do next.

If you find this difficult, start with just two simple tasks back-to-back; after doing that for one week without fail, add a third task, do that for a week, and then continue to add tasks until you are happy with your morning/evening/midday routine.

MODULE 5

THE NEXT CHAPTER

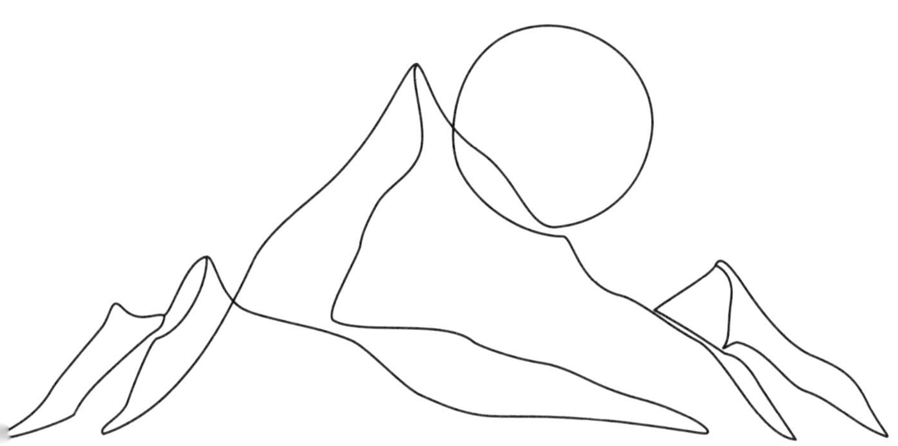

Welcome to module five. In this last module of the book, I will be covering ways that you can implement everything we have learned so far, as well as some new tools, into your life in a practical way, and use these tools on an ongoing basis to chase change. These thirty days are only the beginning of this journey, and over the following six chapters, I want you to see how it is possible to have what you want in the present moment while working towards what you want in your future, creating a balanced and fulfilled life for yourself. As you now know, change is inevitable, so let's get comfortable with the ever-evolving journey.

5.1 What does happiness really mean?

Let's talk about creating real, lasting change in order to enjoy the life we have while we are here. Is lasting happiness possible? Is it really within our grasp to have underlying happiness throughout the ups and downs of our everyday life? The answer is yes. It is possible even if you have never had it before, or if you are someone who feels like happiness is fleeting and hard to maintain.

Happiness can feel like such a difficult goal to achieve because you cannot see it, and it is hard to measure. It's there one day and the next it may not be. So the goal of being happy, as nice as it sounds, can seem complicated and out of reach. Have you asked yourself, *What does it mean to me to be happy?* What is your take on this? You may see it as something that will happen once you have achieved a milestone, or start earning enough money, or once you have your own home, or can retire; then you can be happy. But this is a common misconception. Happiness is a feeling that can exist independent of these external factors.

And there is a science behind it, a method to finally have what seems to be always a step ahead. Let's begin with something called hedonic adaptation (also referred to as the hedonic treadmill). A paper by Diener, Lucas, and Scollon was published in 2006 called 'Beyond the hedonic treadmill', which refers to the idea that after a positive or negative event in your life, you will still ultimately return to your baseline level of affect (aka happiness).[1] Which means that no matter what happens, good or bad, after some time has passed, you will return to what your standard was. Many of us think that if we won the lottery, it would make us happy forever. Our financial stressors would go away, and we would be free and content. On the flip side, we think that if something negative happened, like a major accident that rendered us unable to walk, or losing our job or career, or having the love of our life abandon us, this would leave us destroyed and unable to recover emotionally.

However, this model suggests that these major highs and lows eventually fade, and after more time has passed, you are back where you were before the event. One particular study by Brickman et al. called 'Lottery winners and accident victims: is happiness relative?' showed that months after winning the lottery, people were no happier than the comparison group that were in the lottery who did not win, and no happier than before they won the lottery.[2] They had a temporary spike in happiness, and then it dropped back down. The same went for people going though divorce and other hard life events. After more time, they were back to their original level of happiness, even if the event itself, like a divorce, had lifelong impact.

This proves that the belief that happiness is found in obtaining possessions, money, or status is a fallacy. No one big event will turn your lifelong happiness around. You can spend your entire life on this 'treadmill', chasing that thing that is always in front of you and never in reach, when the potential for a good life was in your grasp all along. This is not to say that you shouldn't try to achieve big goals, but it is important to reframe them.

Hedonic adaptation means that we eventually adapt to what was once exciting. We get over the thrill and are back to where we were. If you are someone who is generally happy, your excitement returns back to that content state, but if you are someone generally negative or unhappy, that returns too. You adapt to the highs and lows, and these major events do not create permanent change.

Look at people who have money, status, and fame, something a lot of people would love to obtain, because they think it is the recipe for a happy life. These people at the so-called 'top' have the same struggles with happiness, if not more than everyone else. And if you are someone that thinks, *What do they have to complain about? They have everything!* then it means you might not have an understanding of what true happiness is. You are still in the mindset of perceiving happiness as something that is derived from the outside. As Jim Carrey says, 'I think everybody should get rich and famous and do everything they ever dreamed of so they can see that it's not the answer.' So many people get to what they think is the holy grail, only to find that happiness is not there. It has to be created within.

I'll give you a more personal example: my sister was an elite athlete for years, competing in rowing, cycling, and even bobsleigh for Australia. When she was younger, heavily involved in cycling, she felt a lot of pressure to win. She had to win at all costs, because it would mean she had achieved what she had set out to do, she would make those who helped her get there proud, and she would finally feel happy. And she did win, many times. But because the pressure was so great – not wanting to let others down, not wanting to think about the repercussions if she did not win – that happiness from the win was never really felt. She describes it to me as this cycle where, after a loss, she would finally get to the top and win, and she would feel relief above anything else. She was trapped in a loop of not enjoying the process because she was so fixated on the outcome. When the outcome didn't go her way, it explained why she was not happy, and when it did go her way, it was just a relief that she didn't let herself or anyone else down. This feeling of happiness that she thought could be derived from winning kept evading her. It did not exist.

After a few years out of sport, she returned to compete in weightlifting, CrossFit, and bobsleigh with a completely new attitude. Instead of being motivated by the outcome of beating everyone else, she decided to become process driven and intrinsically motivated (which is to do something for the inherent satisfaction of doing it, not for the outcome). She focused on the small wins she could create, the ritual of training, the bonding with her teammates and even her competitors, the sense of community, and the improvements in her own physical and mental strength. And suddenly it all turned around. Her drive was as great as ever, but she began to love every moment of it, breaking out of her anxious cycle. And if there was a win at the end, it was just a nice bonus. The real prize was that she had found a way to love what she did. So much so that when she competes now, I see her cheer on her competitors as hard as she would cheer for her own team. When she sees a competitor beat her, she is proud of them like a proud mum, and can authentically celebrate it. Not winning does not take away from her experience. The happiness and enjoyment come from the journey, from the entire experience, not from one outcome.

So let's talk about the baseline of happiness. If we don't feel generally happy, how do we alter this, without looking for these external sources? And how can we prevent this adaptation to the good things that happen, so that special feeling doesn't start to feel commonplace, and we don't slip back into our old ways?

You can prevent this adaptation to good things happening by learning to incorporate two things:

1. Variety
2. Appreciation

A good example of using variety to overcome adaptation applies to music, when you've just discovered a new song you love. I think it's safe to say we have all been there. You hear a song, it's the best thing ever, like nothing you have heard before. You play it. You *love* it. You play it again straight after. And then you play it so many times that it's no longer that exciting. Eventually you have flogged that song so much you are now bored, or if you took it to the extreme, you can't even listen to it anymore. You did not allow for variety, so you adapted to something very quickly. Additionally, the more you play it, the less likely you are to be in the moment, loving every part of that song as you listen. You did at the start, but then less and less. Lack of variety and appreciation is causing this.

If you play a song you love but mix it up with other things – other songs, podcasts, audiobooks – and drip feed yourself that song as a treat, you are more likely to *never* get over the song, and never end up hating it. You will enjoy it for a lot longer, and appreciate how much you love it when you do listen to it. This way, you stave off this adaptation.

Ensuring that you don't derive all your joy from instant gratification is a great way to include appreciation. You want to be choosing things where the more you do it, the better it feels. Unlike eating sweets, being on social media, or other quick dopamine hits, I'm talking about things like hobbies, engaging in community-driven exercises, etc.

Starting a sport is great for variety. It varies slightly every time, because no two games are exactly alike. There are different things to experience, different conversations; you are always learning, overcoming new challenges, and you see growth.

Effort also plays a big role in avoiding this kind of adaptation. Finishing something that took serious effort gives us a lot of happiness while providing constant evolution in what we are doing. Make sure it is realistic effort where you can overcome challenges and still see progress. Not instant gratification, and nothing so hard you get nowhere and are hitting your head against a wall.

Another way to look at things you enjoy is to ask yourself: Is this like cake, or sport? Imagine you are about to eat a cake, or anything sweet you like. The first bite is amazing, it's exciting, you've been looking forward to this treat for hours. The second bite is almost as good. The third is good, but not as good, and then you start adapting to it. Then all of a sudden it does not make you happy anymore: *Get it away, I'm too full!* Sport, on the other hand, can offer community, variety, challenges, effort, and excitement. The same initial spark is there, but you don't hate it after a few times. Notice the difference between both forms of something that creates joy. One is sustainable, the other is not.

So when you think about happiness, bring it back to smaller picture things. It's never going to come from that big milestone you have your mind set on, as important as those milestones are. Think of variety and appreciation for what is happening in the moment. Be grateful for what the journey is providing you now, not what that future thing will provide you later.

Additional resources

For more on this topic, I'd recommend the books *The Subtle Art of Not Giving a F*ck*, by Mark Manson, and *Learned Optimism*, by Martin Seligman.

5.2 Self-directed neuroplasticity: it's not what you can do, it's what you will do.

Neuroplasticity. This term is about as exciting as it sounds, but it is important to know what it really means when you hear about the concept of creating neuroplastic changes in the brain. What is neuroplasticity, exactly? It is the ability of the brain to create, organise, and reorganise synaptic connections (and in some areas of the brain, to form new neurons). This happens in response to experiences, learning, or after injury or trauma. It is essentially how your brain responds and adapts to any stimulus, and, depending on how severe or repetitive the stimulus is, will determine how much change occurs.

It's important to note that not all neuroplasticity is a good thing. The brain reorganises itself in response to a stimulus, good or bad. If you have emotional trauma, your brain will learn to operate in a different way to someone who does not. You will lean into more protective, fearful behaviours, and it will alter how you interpret situations and how you feel about your own abilities. However, on the flip side, learning a skill, trying new things, and training the brain to do something specific with intention can reorganise pathways in the brain to make it work for you. The term 'plastic' basically refers to being changeable.

Self-directed neuroplasticity is exactly that: it is where *you*, the individual, are the one directing this change intentionally, unlike the broader term, where the environment can direct this change. In this case, the mind (thoughts, emotions, etc.) has the ability to change the brain's function and structure. This type of neuroplasticity is what allows the brain to overcome old habits and maladaptive responses to create new ways of behaving, thinking, reasoning, and even feeling.

Don't fall for the trap of thinking that when you are less stressed or when you are happier, you will be able to overcome things more easily, waiting for things to change before taking action. Instead, it is the other way around. When you put tools in place to manage stress and difficult situations, your brain will adapt to how you approach things, and you will deal with them more productively, which will then improve your mood. You want to tackle things from every angle, not just those things that are happening outside of you but what is happening inside the brain as well. Remember what we learned about LTP (long-term potentiation): cells that fire together, wire together.

Until the 1960s, it was generally believed that the brain would be able to change throughout childhood and adolescence, but when it reached adulthood, it would become relatively fixed in its ways. Researchers also thought that neurogenesis (the birth of new neurons) stopped soon after birth. Now we know that is not the case. The brain actually has two kinds of neuroplasticity available to it throughout our lives: functional and structural.

Functional neuroplasticity is where the brain has the ability to shift the function from a damaged area of the brain to an undamaged area to take over. This can be seen in patients that have experienced brain trauma or disease (more on this in my recommended reading at the end of this chapter). Structural neuroplasticity, on the other hand, is what is happening when you're utilising self-directed neuroplasticity. This is where physical structures within the brain are altered because of learning something new.

An example of self-directed neuroplasticity is what happens when you change how you speak to yourself and treat yourself: your self-esteem goes up, and you are willing to start to attempt things. Then you see progress and attempt even more, and you slowly start to change how your brain functions as a result of changing how you think about yourself. This can be done by overriding old thoughts with new thoughts, overriding old statements with new statements. Many of the exercises in this book are based around this principle, but to really drive home this example, I want to share with you a story sent to me by one of my podcast listeners that shows how you can create change in your life by creating changes within your thinking and beliefs.

A longtime listener wrote to me explaining the massive change she had created for herself by making small changes within herself. She told me that two years ago when she started listening to my podcast, she was in an emotionally abusive marriage, extremely unhappy in a job she hated, and raising three children. She felt trapped with nowhere to turn, wanting to change her circumstances while protecting her kids. She discovered my podcast and would listen to it in secrecy (so her husband would not know). She ordered my first book and had it delivered to her work so it would not be found at home. Slowly, she realised she could start making real change by changing how she thought about her situation. There *was* something she could do, no matter how small. Once her mindset began to shift, she started taking one workday a week to study in preparation for a job change, and in under one year, she had left home, gotten a placement in her new career, and was able to leave the marriage with her children. She wrote to me saying that they were not just surviving, now they were now thriving.

She went from feeling trapped, feeling like there was no way out, to true freedom and happiness, and it only took one small spark: the idea of making a change in thought before it could crystallise in action. She realised change was possible, which is the first and biggest step for many. Because she finally saw change as a possibility, she started to see where she could take some power back in her life.

She started with one thing: listening to something that made her feel better. The next step felt bigger, but possible, which was ordering the book. These seemingly tiny actions speak volumes when you are making self-directed changes within the brain. You start to demonstrate to yourself that you are not only worth the effort but capable. It makes doing the next thing possible too, like enrolling in her dream course. She changed how she spoke to herself, how she viewed her future, and what she would be capable of achieving, and she stopped looking at herself as helpless. In such a short timeframe, she transformed her life to one beyond what she thought was possible.

That is the beauty of self-directed change. It's like an itch; you just need to start to scratch it and it becomes difficult to stop. You start with small changes, and once you realise how impactful they are, you become hooked on the feeling of knowing you have control over so much. Before you know it, the goals you're setting for yourself are ones that one year ago, you would never have dreamed of or imagined. Every time you see yourself in a position that feels hopeless, ask yourself, *Is this* really *the limit to what I can experience here? Is there the possibility of change?* The moment you see something as adaptable and not a dead end is the moment you become proactive and not reactive, and that is when change starts to happen. Start to question things you are unhappy with, talking to yourself in a new way, and see where it takes you.

Additional resource

The Brain That Changes Itself, by Norman Doidge, is one of the books that solidified my love for neuroscience. This book will give you a fascinating insight into how plastic the brain can really be when it comes to healing, covering numerous stories of personal triumph. Seeing how the brain can achieve so much in the case studies of the book will inspire you to imagine what your own brain has the capacity to do.

5.3 Reputation: what will you be known for?

Reputation is one of my favourite topics. When you think about reputation, you think, *What am I known for?* And this reputation doesn't materialise out of nowhere; it's formed over time; it is the sum of all your past actions and determines how others will interact with you and how you will be treated. We all have many reputations that represent our past patterns of behaviour up until now. Some of these are great, and maybe there are some you would like to change. Reputation can be based around personality traits (for example, the loud one, the last one standing on a night out, the homebody, the serious one) and, of course, behaviours (for example, always late, always cancels last minute, unreliable, always quits, a person of their word, so generous, so caring and nurturing, etc.).

The beauty of reputation is that it cannot be bought, borrowed, stolen, or faked. It's all about track record. It is inherently honest. It also must be observed by others; your telling someone something repeatedly is not enough. Others need to see your actions or be on the receiving end of them to cement your status. Good reputations are easy to break, and bad reputations are very hard to outrun. If you have a reputation of never cheating, and one time, you cheat on a test, you have damaged your reputation. However, if you are always late, and you arrive early one time, that's not enough to change your reputation, because there needs to be consistency in order for people to see positive change.

Reputation is also important because it is often how you learn about other people. When you start dating someone or meet a new friend, you may hear things about them that will affect how you enter the relationship. And when you judge someone, it is often due to their reputation. You either agree with what you've heard, or you don't. Trust is built on reputation, because it takes a while to earn a good one. Having a good reputation is what will get you connections, professional opportunities, contacts, networks, and healthy relationships.

So, how do you change a reputation? You have to replace that behaviour with a different one and be consistent. If you want to be known to be adventurous, it requires a track record of being out there and trying new things. Doing something once is 'out of character'; doing something enough times will gain you a reputation.

I also want to point out that there is an important difference between wanting to have a certain reputation in the eyes of those around you, and living to please others. While 'people-pleasing' is not a clinical or medical term, it's a common label referring to people who will constantly try to please other people, often at the expense of their own needs or desires. A lot of people pleasers do this to feel accepted or loved, and if they fail to please others, they feel it may negatively impact people's perception of them (even if that is not the case at all). Yes, reputation is based on how others perceive you, but you do not do it for the sole purpose of pleasing, while not feeling fulfilled yourself.

Your reputation should also represent your own values and morals, showing others what it means to live by your own standards. Reputation is a very close reflection of what you value highly in your life. So, as you mature and evolve, often your reputation does, too. A good exercise is to look back five or ten years and see how your behaviours and things you are known for have evolved as you have grown, and what factors were responsible for that. Normally, taking on a huge responsibility is a catalyst for change, like a big job opportunity, a child, or, unfortunately, a health condition. Some things can be so big, they cause change overnight. But it is also possible to begin to change on your own. Chasing change for yourself causes you to change your reputation at the same time.

Your reputation in your own eyes is just as important as what others think of you. It is about making a promise to yourself and honouring that promise, creating a new track record for yourself. It is defining what you value first, and then having your pattern of behaviours level up to meet those values. It is integrity. Confidence in yourself and your own abilities is something you build on, and you start doing this by following through with the kinds of changes and small daily habits we've been discussing throughout this book. How can you be confident in your own ability, if you cannot trust that you will follow through with something that you want to be known for? Once you start following through on small promises to yourself, it becomes easier to feel confident in setting bigger goals and promises, because you have built a reputation of being true to your word. That is how you start to trust yourself to make big changes long-term.

Personally, I used to have a reputation as an asthmatic who could not exercise. This will probably surprise you, as I've told you all about the daily fitness regimen I stick to now. But for years and years I opted out of any kind of exercise that required running because I believed it would bring on an asthma attack, and it often did when I was very young. As a teen, I was that student who hated physical education classes, as I rarely got involved in any cardio – except for swimming, which the doctor said was great for me. But one day at my job, when I was around twenty-one years old, a bunch of people were forming a group for a 10K fun run. They decided they would train twice a week in the four months leading up to the event as a team-building exercise. I really wanted to join them, and deep down I had always loved the idea of running. And even though my asthma had improved drastically since I was a child, I never gave it a go, even as a teen or into adulthood. This time I thought, *Why not? People with asthma do this shit all the time, why can't I at least try?* So I started training, extremely slowly, with my asthma meds in hand, and four months later, I completed the 10K fun run.

Now I run two 10Ks per week, have run a few half-marathons, and even have a goal to run a full marathon someday. And when I talk to people about it, I often hear, 'I could never do that! It's easier for you because you're a runner; some people are just built to run.' I have changed my reputation so much in that area that most people have no idea I was this PE-hating child who would run fifty metres and get an asthma attack, a far cry from someone who is 'built to run'. I love seeing how I was able to completely change this reputation for myself, to the extent that people are shocked to hear I would opt out of PE class back in the day. It is so ingrained in me now, people presume I grew up behaving this way.

You can turn almost anything around and create a new reputation, for your health, your work ethic, your fitness levels, and even your intelligence. This is a huge one, as many people believe your intellectual ability is fixed and cannot change. You hear it everywhere in the way people talk about themselves, or even children: 'They are so smart, I am not intelligent,' or 'I am not book smart, I'm really bad academically.' It is spoken about as if it is an unchangeable genetic trait, like eye colour. But intelligence is *not* fixed. Almost anyone willing to put in the work will be very surprised at how much they can gain. But, like any other story we tell ourselves, it is a catch-22. If you believe it is not in you, you never really try, because in your mind there is a ceiling. So your attempts will be with minimal effort, because why bother, right? You then use this fixed mindset idea (like we spoke about earlier), and you bring in confirmation bias to think of all the times your intelligence has not been what you wanted it to be, never looking at examples where you have learned something new. The simple act of challenging this belief is enough to start turning around how you approach not just intelligence but any skill you would like to earn and obtain. It starts with critical thinking and challenging your belief. Ask yourself, *Why do I think this is true, and how can I prove this belief wrong?*

Don't be embarrassed to start making these changes. Yes, people may be surprised at first, and may say that what you are doing is 'out of character'. It may be out of character for your *old* self, but it is very aligned with the character of your new self, and soon enough it won't seem strange. Other people take time to adapt, and don't let people's resistance to change be the reason you do not chase change for yourself. Change is inevitable, so you may as well be the one creating it.

Your daily task

So, what do you want your reputation to be? And are you even clear on what your reputation is currently? Write down what you think it is and also what you would love for it to be. Or better yet, talk to some people you trust, and ask them to dish out all the good and bad things that you are known for. How would they describe you to others when you are not there? Even better: talk to friends who've known you a long time, so they can help you reflect on ways your reputation has evolved. This is a great way of seeing how you come across in the eyes of others. If you can do this with a handful of people, then you will start to see some common themes. And if there is something you don't like, it can be changed.

5.4 Change is an inevitable part of life. Embrace it.

Imagine this. You have worked hard to get to where you want to be. You are thirty, living in your own home in a certain city, with your routines, working away at your career, and suddenly, you have a realisation that you want something else. You want a different life than the one you have made for yourself. But you think to yourself, you are already thirty – it feels too late to start all over again. What do you do? Stay, knowing that there is something else that is your thing, that you could really sink your teeth into, a different life? Or would you take the leap?

We have this idea that starting over is the worst-case scenario. But starting over happens many times in your life. Life is cyclical, things come in waves: careers, goals, family, relationships all evolve and evolve again. So to think you have to stay in something because it is the status quo is to go against the nature of life, which is driven by constant change.

Yes, you may try to create change and find that it does not go the way you planned. Not everything does. You will not always make the correct decisions in life, and what sometimes starts off as the right decision evolves into something that no longer works for you. What you once loved, you have grown out of. But the objective here is to learn to be okay with outgrowing certain decisions, beliefs, and relationships. Life is a series of never-ending contrasts. You know what you want because you have experienced what you don't want. And this understanding, these lessons in life, help to guide you.

Another problem may be that you are terrified to start over because you are constantly comparing your timeline to those around you. This comparison of timelines has so much power over people's decisions about their own lives. When you live by a timeline, and everyone around you is hitting milestones that you think you need to be hitting, then starting over feels like the worst-case scenario. Even if you are miserable with the life you have, it still feels terrifying to throw it away because of that comparison. But I can assure you, the moment you start living a life exploring the things you want to explore, doing what you want to do, working towards something that really matters to you, everything else goes out the window, and comparison fades away. You do not compare yourself to others when you are satisfied, even if you are at a starting point. Because your happiness is no longer based on external milestones, but, instead, on intrinsic things that you do for the sake of the process, not the outcome.

And a lot of these external markers of success will be things you do not have direct control over. That is why you need to look inward and think, *What can I focus on right now that I am happy about within myself?* When you do this, you are less likely to think, *Oh, I'm in this place in my life but my friend just purchased a house! And I can't afford a house right now at my age!* All this quiets down when we look inward. The more you find passion in what you do (whether it is linked to career or not), the less you care about where you are in life in comparison to those around you.

This is the reason a lot of people choose to not start again, in relationships, and in careers. People will literally be miserable and stay in a life situation where they are not maximising their potential because they do not want to appear to have fallen behind on this timeline that we call life. They do not want to feel like they have had all this loss and no gain. We have these arbitrary dates in our head of when we have to achieve all these milestones, but where does the milestone of happiness slot in there? When should we have achieved peace? Or personal fulfilment? You can get so busy comparing timelines, you forget to ask yourself if you are actually happy, even when you are 'keeping up' with the crowd.

I'm here to tell you it is always okay to start over. And making big decisions later in life can actually be a blessing in disguise and work out for the better. Sometimes you need time or life experience to be able to start something, that maybe you could never have started had you done it earlier in your life. Lessons and experiences can always be applied to your next chapter. What you've been through is never a waste.

I changed my life at thirty, and I am actually glad it did not happen earlier, because every other attempt at something else contributed to the decisions I was making at that time. My idea of what I want in life has changed so many times so far, I don't think I could count them all. And most of them failed. I remember getting to the end of my twenty-ninth year, thinking I was getting old, and comparing myself to all my close girlfriends. Some of them had purchased a home, others were getting promoted, getting engaged, having children, starting businesses and succeeding, quitting their full-time jobs because their side hustles were doing so well, etc. And here I was, fresh out of a breakup and heartbroken. I couldn't afford the bond payment to rent a bedroom in a share house and had to borrow money for it. I was working as a Pilates cover instructor because I had no permanent shifts, felt no security with where my money was coming from and had just returned from overseas, so practically everything I owned could fit into two suitcases. It was a tough time for my identity, because I was too tempted to compare myself to others. I was about to turn thirty. Isn't that the time you are supposed to have it all worked out? It felt like my twenties had been a series of attempts at new things that resulted in my feeling behind all my friends in my circle. I don't normally feel anxious, but I can definitely say this was very anxiety provoking for me. And when I look back to dissect that feeling, it was because I was not doing anything that made me excited, that I could sink my teeth into and pour effort into, where I could see growth. The moment I started studying, doing the podcast, doing things that leaned into my interests (with no idea where they would get me in the long run), I stopped focusing on what everyone else was doing. I stopped comparing myself well before I was making more money or building a relationship or any of the things my friends were already doing.

What I thought I wanted was all the milestones that my friends were hitting. What I actually *needed* was to be happy with myself. When I created that happiness, the need for the external things I 'had to have' faded away. Those things are independent of your happiness. Listen to yourself and your interests, and lean into that no matter what. If you know you are ready for change, you must chase it, because change is inevitable.

There should be no aim to reach an end point. You should always be growing and evolving. Don't plan on achieving all your goals at any given time, because your ideas, plans, and goals keep evolving as you do. I like knowing I always have things to work towards; I like knowing I am a work in progress.

As humans we love to learn and evolve, and part of that is not having to have it all figured out. Or maybe having it figured out just means knowing that life is about progress, not the end point. And once you reach that place, you become more process driven, not end-result driven. There should be no exact finish line, so don't rush to it, because it would just be wishing your time away. Find something you love and throw yourself into it, and then, when something changes – and something always changes – go ahead and find it again.

Additional resources

For more on this topic, I'd recommend the book *Take the Leap,* by Sara Bliss, which features inspiring stories and advice from more than sixty-five people who transformed their lives, often by changing careers to pursue their passions. These examples are a ton of fun, and really illustrate that it's never too late to make a change.

5.5 The neuroscience of willpower.

Welcome to the second-to-last day of your thirty-day journey to master your mindset. As we're wrapping up, I think it's important to cover the topic of willpower, and what happens in the brain when you choose to commit to something. There are so many people out there who pick up a great self-help book or learn amazing tips from something they've read or heard, but then before they know it, they're back to square one, hardly remembering this new information. And you've come too far on this thirty-day journey to be one of these people! I want you to harness the willpower to continue chasing change long after you've finished this book.

If you are anything like me (and I presume you are, because you are reading this), then you want to know what is happening in the brain behind the scenes that's causing things to be easy or difficult as you work on these exercises to implement change. And when I learned about the neuroscience of willpower, it allowed me to understand so much about how you can increase your drive and your level of commitment.

Let's chat about commitment for a second. A commitment is an agreement or a pledge. It is also a choice. When you commit to doing something and follow through with that task, it says something about your integrity, because it was a choice you made to follow through. If you had no choice but to do something, then it was not really a commitment. Most people will only tackle an essay or large task days before it is due because they do not want to fail the subject or miss the deadline and suffer the repercussions in the long run. So, this becomes a situation where they have less of a choice, or the negative repercussions are such that they now have to take action to avoid them. But these incentives also serve a very strong purpose, because they teach you what you are truly capable of. Sometimes it is important to be put under this kind of pressure to gain insight into the limits to your performance and where they can be pushed. If you did not have these in place, would you be self-driven enough to do these things? (Thinking back to my university days, I don't think I would have, so I am a big fan of a deadline here and there to test my skills.)

So, what is happening in the brain when you do hard things? Why is it that some people seem to be able to do these uncomfortable tasks repeatedly or administer crazy levels of self-control, and others struggle to follow through on the things they said they would do? Well, it turns out there is a specific part of the brain that is responsible for, or at least heavily involved in, willpower, or your willingness to do things.

This area is called the anterior mid-cingulate cortex (AMCC). This is the region in the brain that is directly involved with willpower and tenacity, and the more you engage in difficult tasks, or tasks that require 'motivation' or effort, the larger this area becomes. It literally grows in size. This is another great example of self-directed neuroplasticity that we spoke about a few chapters ago. Physical changes are occurring in the brain as a direct result of your effort. And the beauty of it is that this neuroplastic change is always available to you. If you are someone who thinks, *I have no self-control, it's hard for me to see things through, I'm not like other people*, know that it will not be like that forever. It will suck at the start. Doing these hard things will feel insurmountable (which is why you start small, like I explained in the habit creation section), but because you are creating change on a *physical* level in the brain, it *will* become easier. Your willingness to do something will increase.

People with a larger AMCC are not born this way; the increase in size is all self-directed. If you can push past the threshold and train your brain like a muscle, then you can perform better, just like training a muscle in a gym. You use it, it works for you. You don't use it, you lose it.

People who follow things through, who finish what they start, who are people of their word, have an ingrained belief that they have what it takes to get the job done, to complete that task. That is where willpower comes in. It is thinking, *This will require effort that I am willing to give.* And in people who rarely do difficult things, or have little self-control – that is, the inability to say no, to reign it in, to go home when they said they would go home, to resist temptation – that region in the brain is smaller.

Like we learned early on in this book, we humans are more likely to be motivated *not* to lose something than by the possibility of gaining something else. This can help you structure ways to learn to stick something out. For example, when I book a class at my yoga studio, I go even if I am not in the mood, because I would get charged an extra twenty dollars on top of my membership for a no-show. This is a great motivator for many people. However, if someone said, *I'll give you twenty dollars* extra *to go to that class*, I may turn it down, even though I would be in a better position financially. This is how we are wired, and it is a great insight to help us structure reward versus penalty for ourselves when learning to increase our willpower.

You also want to factor in the cost-benefit computation that you need in order to have strong willpower. We all place a cost on something. And that cost will vary for each individual based on their perspective. This is where you can separate wanting something versus being willing to do something, as they are very, very different. You could want to be a doctor, imagining the kind of life you would have and thinking it could tap into all your interests, *but* the cost might be too high. Maybe the years to sacrifice in med school are too much, maybe you would be missing out on things that matter to you (the fun part of your twenties, for instance, or time with family). Maybe you know how hard you'd have to study, and know the thousands of hours involved, so you weigh up the cost and the benefit and you make the call not to do it. Now, this is an extreme example, but you do this with everyday things as well.

Look at running a marathon: a lot of people would love the idea of having run one, but look at the cost involved, and for them, it simply does not weigh up against the benefit. For many, it is just not worth the hours of training and the gruelling marathon itself.

To get even more granular, the cost of not drinking alcohol leads to the benefit of waking up feeling fresh the next day so you can go do your favourite spin class. But the other cost might be not having a fun late night out. So for some, that cost is too high. They value the late night out drinking over the early-morning feeling. And it's not until the next day that you think, *Wow, I am never drinking again.*

So what is it that you want, and what is the cost? And now, knowing the cost, can you afford it? Is it worth the benefit? How does it weigh up for you? The more you engage in hard things, the more you are able to spend (in energy, time, focus, attention, and restraint) to get that reward.

That is when you know you really want something. You are able to look at the cost and say it is *still* worth it. Hopefully, the exercises in this book so far have helped you get clearer on your short- and long-term goals, and the true costs of achieving them. When you find something that's worth the effort, when you are still willing to do something despite the cost involved, then you should go all-in, because it's a rare indicator of something truly important to you.

Your daily task

Write down a few things you have wanted but not followed through with in your life, and then next to each one, write down what the cost would have been for you to complete that. Then, write down a few more things you *have* completed and achieved, and what cost you had to invest to achieve them.

Can you dissect this in order to understand what it is that you are willing to do versus not willing to do? What kinds of goals are you valuing more than others, and why? Do you think that the cost of certain things is too high because you do not have practice in administering willpower? (If this is the case, then it may be a goal still worth pursuing.) Or do you think you didn't do it because you simply do not see the value in the reward versus cost (which is also a good thing to acknowledge)?

5.6 The deathbed test.

Have you ever felt paralysed by making a choice? Whenever you are unsure what to do, whether it's a big decision or you're just wondering how you should structure your day, then try doing the deathbed test. It's a way of putting yourself in the shoes of your future self in a very emotional way. The idea is that you are standing at the end of your life, with the ability to look back and decide if something was worth it or not. What would your future self want from you in this moment?

How many times would you wish that you had taken that leap of faith, stood up for yourself, dumped that arsehole who treated you like crap, said what you really meant, defended someone you cared about, chose what you wanted over what was expected of you, not stayed in a situation just because you were afraid of being judged for quitting, or expressed yourself instead of staying quiet? I think we can all relate to at least one of these feelings. And pinpointing these moments is a great way of helping us make a decision for our current self.

The deathbed test helps you put things into perspective. When all is said and done, when the years have passed, will my reason not to do something still matter? Will I still be happy with my decision? This is one of the best ways to get myself to not waste time or procrastinate, and to clarify what I really want.

My sister was the one who introduced me to this test, and she took it a step further. She went out and purchased a poster with small circles that represent each day of your life, if you were to live to be ninety. This poster is filled with thousands of tiny circles. The circles or days you have already lived get coloured in, and the empty ones are what is ahead of you. She says that when she sees that poster each morning, it is a reminder to maximise her time, and to maximise each day. A few people have asked her, *Doesn't that make you sad? Focusing on how many days are left, the number always getting smaller?* And she says it has the opposite effect for her. That it puts her in a good mood, because it brings all the important things to the forefront, and all the insignificant things that she should not be worried about seem small and don't consume her day.

This test has helped me make really difficult decisions in my life: leaving jobs and careers I loved, to take a risk on something I wanted more; leaving relationships that were not right, even though I was terrified; going on adventures even though I would have to give up something else, even when there was no guarantee things would work out. And the biggest one has been putting myself out there when I may embarrass myself. When I start something new, I will always ask myself, *Will these people criticising or judging me or laughing at me be relevant years down the line, and will my fear of their opinions be worth not pursuing something?* The answer has always been no.

This question will set you free time and time again, because it gets right to the bottom of what it is that you truly want, and what you value the most. If you are confused about what your values and morals are, do the test until the answer reveals itself. If you are confused which road to go down, you can always come back to this question.

This again is where regret comes in handy. It is a guide for your future. As we discussed in module two, I don't normally like to sit in regret, and actually think the word's used too often where it shouldn't apply. However, if it does arise, I turn it into something useful – otherwise, what's the point? Regret serves as a teacher, as an alarm bell, as a warning sign for your future self. If you say, 'I regret not going on that trip!' then next time you are faced with an opportunity, you know what it feels like to say no. If you regret not being honest, this is your push to speak your truth the next time you have the opportunity, because you know you would rather face the discomfort in the moment than carry the regret into the future. And after the regret has served as a lesson, I do not regret the thing in the past anymore, because I know it helped me on my journey forward. Even the things you wish you didn't do can serve their purpose if you learn from them. It does not have to be a waste.

I know it can be hard to maintain this outlook, given that we all have limited time on this earth. Dr William Breitbart is a renowned psychiatrist who has done a lot of work on mortality and helping people find meaning in their life. He's developed a practice called 'meaning-centred psychotherapy', which is used to sustain meaning and spiritual health in terminally ill patients – things which he's found are major factors in their sense of suffering.[1] He talks about how it influences your life, and the responsibility you have to be authentic in your life in every moment and in every action. He says that death is a call to life.

It is common to go through life feeling as though we need to have certain things, for these goals on our list to happen so we can finally be happy, be at peace, or finally feel fulfilled. We think that only then, when we have everything we wanted, can we relax, soak up the little moments, and find joy in the every day. People will hustle so hard striving for this feeling. But the feeling is created internally, and no external endeavor will create that for you. You already have that within you.

And it actually happens the other way around. When you discover your own happiness and create peace for your mind in each day, you can focus on the details and get clear on what you really want. And it is in the details, the small habits, the tiny improvements, the progress you notice at work, in your health, in your body, the moments of connection, the laughter, the hugs, the moments patting your dog or enjoying the feeling of getting into bed that, when added up, equal an amazing life. And it is also these small moments that lead you to the bigger moments. If you try to bypass these small wins, you will be holding yourself in a place where things are not happening for you, and you're feeling restricted. If you get involved in these small moments, they will be the steps that will naturally lead you to the bigger things. But you cannot have one without the other.

And when you focus on these daily joys, all the things you thought you had to have in order to be happy no longer seem so crucial. And because there is no longer this desperation to have them, since you have already become the source of your own happiness, those things will enter your life a whole lot more easily, because your approach has changed. You go from blocking and getting in your own way to allowing space, making connections, creating opportunities, and things seem to come your way effortlessly, but it's not magic. You are in a better headspace, and you are more aware of the opportunities and people around you. Your focus is higher, and your effort is greater.

Train your brain to look for the good. The more you do it, the easier it becomes. Looking at one thing that frustrates you can very easily lead you to more things that do. That is why when you have reached your capacity for patience, someone can do something that normally wouldn't annoy you, and it will send you over the edge. The same can go for positive thoughts. The more you accumulate and recognise these thoughts, the easier it is to draw in more of the same, and before you know it, you are in a state when something annoying can happen to you and you didn't even notice, or it even made you smile or laugh. Perception is everything, and how you guide your mind to perceive what is happening around you is within your control. What you choose to focus on – your mindset – will determine the quality and trajectory of your life.

Your daily task

For the last task of these thirty days, I would love for you to take a moment and reflect on everything you have absorbed and learned about yourself. It is always important to pause and reflect every so often, to check in with yourself at different stages of your journey.

You have done many different tasks, some of which I hope are now a part of your lifestyle, and others that you will put into practice soon. Which parts of the book resonated with you? Which chapters do you want to return to so you can master that topic? I will sometimes revisit a chapter as many times as I need to so it can be solidified in my head.

Lastly, I want you to write out on a piece of paper what your future life could look like in twelve months' time. Write every aspect in as much detail as you can, from your morning routine to your physical health, to your night-time habits, your relationships, your happiness, your achievements big and small. Now, take that piece of paper and place it somewhere safe, and set a reminder for yourself to look at that paper again in one year. This note, this idea of your future, will be in the back of your mind, and you will feel more motivated to follow through with the hard tasks and push through the discomfort in order to meet that version of yourself in twelve months, and know you did something for yourself. Do this task today, and do your future self a favour.

Conclusion

Congratulations on getting to the end of this thirty-day journey. My hope is that you are feeling empowered and more in control than ever of your life, your happiness, and your future. I want you to remember that your journey is not linear; there will always be peaks and valleys, but what is constant is that change is inevitable. Your role is to deal with changes that come your way and create new change for yourself, so you are not at the mercy of what happens around you but always in the driver's seat.

Life is always unfolding. It is not a destination, and if you look at it that way, you'll always have that sense of 'now what?' when you reach a milestone or change. A fulfilled life is not about ticking off every goal; it is you, a work in progress, creating happiness, connection, growth, and purpose, not waiting for these things to happen to you.

Lastly, I want you to remember that we are all at a different point in our lives. Some people have it easier than you, some have it harder. But starting worse off than those around you is never a reason not to give yourself a chance. Every single person, no matter their starting point, is able to improve their life. You are able to direct your life to a better place, which then makes it easier to go to the next level, and then the next. But it all starts with a decision. That decision is to chase change, and not let change chase you.

Endnotes

1.2 What is your purpose? Do you really need one?

1 Stacey M Schaefer, Jennifer Morozink Boylan, Carien M van Reekum, Regina C Lapate, Catherine J Norris, Carol D Ryff, Richard J Davidson. 'Purpose in Life Predicts Better Emotional Recovery from Negative Stimuli', *PLOS One*, vol. 8, no. 11, (2013).

2 David R Cregg, Jennifer S Cheavens. 'Healing through helping: an experimental investigation of kindness, social activities, and reappraisal as well-being interventions', *The Journal of Positive Psychology*, vol. 18, no. 6, (2022).

2.2 Why do you block yourself from living the life you want?

1 Jayme R McReynolds, Christa K McIntyre. 'Emotional modulation of the synapse', *Reviews in the Neurosciences*, vol. 23, no. 5–6, (2012).

2.5 Choose a growth mindset over a fixed mindset.

1 'Decades of Scientific Research that Started a Growth Mindset Revolution', *Mindset Works*, https://www.mindsetworks.com/science/. Accessed 28 January 2025.

2 Rachel E White, Emily O Prager, Catherine Schaefer, Ethan Kross, Angela L Duckworth, Stephanie M Carlson. 'The "Batman Effect": Improving Perseverance in Young Children', *Child Development*, vol. 88, no. 5, (2017).

3.4 Understand the value you provide and receive.

1 Zach Brittle, 'Turn Towards Instead of Away', *Gottman*, posted 1 April 2015, https://www.gottman.com/blog/turn-toward-instead-of-away/.

3.5 Maintain your autonomy.

1 Esther S Kluwer, Johan C Karremans, Larisa Riedijk, C Raymond Knee. 'Autonomy in Relatedness: How Need Fulfillment Interacts in Close Relationships', *Personality and Social Psychology Bulletin*, vol. 46, no. 4, (2019).

4.2 Adherence and self-efficacy will help you stick to your goals.

1 Daniel Collado-Mateo, Ana Myriam Lavín-Pérez, Cecilia Peñacoba, Juan Del Coso, Marta Leyton-Román, Antonio Luque-Casado, Pablo Gasque, Miguel Ángel Fernández-del-Olmo, Diana Amado-Alonso. 'Key Factors Associated with

Adherence to Physical Exercise in Patients with Chronic Diseases and Older Adults: An Umbrella Review', *International Journal of Environmental Research and Public Health*, vol. 18, no. 4, (2021).

4.3 Name it to tame it: pushing past discomfort to stay on track.

1 Lisa Firestone, 'Name It to Tame It: The Emotions Underlying Your Triggers', *Psychology Today,* posted 1 February 2022, https://www.psychologytoday.com/us/blog/compassion-matters/202202/name-it-to-tame-it-the-emotions-underlying-your-triggers.

2 Katharina Kircanski, Matthew D Lieberman, Michelle G Craske. 'Feelings into words: contributions of language to exposure therapy', *Psychological Science*, vol. 23, no. 10, (2012).

3 Amber Felton, 'Limbic System: What to Know', *WebMD,* https://www.webmd.com/brain/limbic-system-what-to-know. Accessed 30 January 2025.

4.4 Small time management changes that lead to life-altering habits.

1 Sherri Gordon, 'The Connection Between Cleanliness and Mental Health', *Verywell Mind,* https://www.verywellmind.com/how-mental-health-and-cleaning-are-connected-5097496. Accessed 30 January 2025.

2 Kevin P Madore, Anthony D Wagner. 'Multicosts of Multitasking', *Cerebrum: The Dana Forum on Brain Science*, (2019).

4.5 How to harness dopamine and make it work for you, not against you.

1 'Dopamine', *Cleveland Clinic,* https://my.clevelandclinic.org/health/articles/22581-dopamine. Accessed 30 January 2025.

4.6 Let your results speak for themselves.

1 Marwa Azab, 'Why Sharing Your Goals Makes Them Less Achievable', *Psychology Today,* posted 1 January 2018, https://www.psychologytoday.com/us/blog/neuroscience-in-everyday-life/201801/why-sharing-your-goals-makes-them-less-achievable.

4.7 The truth about discipline and freedom.

1 Mitchell Harper, 'Why Steve Jobs Wore The Same Outfit Everyday', *Inc42,* posted 18 January 2016, https://inc42.com/resources/steve-jobs-outfit/.

2 James Clear, 'How to Build New Habits by Taking Advantage of Old Ones', *James Clear,* https://jamesclear.com/habit-stacking. Accessed 30 January 2025.

5.1 What does happiness really mean?

1 Ed Diener, Richard E Lucas, Christie Napa Scollon. 'Beyond the hedonic treadmill: revising the adaptation theory of well-being', *The American Psychologist*, vol. 61, no. 4, (2006).

2 Philip Brickman, Dan Coates, Ronnie Janoff-Bulman. 'Lottery winners and accident victims: Is happiness relative?', *Journal of Personality and Social Psychology*, vol. 36, no. 8, (1978).

5.6 The deathbed test.

1 Lori P Montross Thomas, Emily A Meier, Scott A Irwin. 'Meaning-Centered Psychotherapy: A Form of Psychotherapy for Patients With Cancer', *Current Psychiatry Reports*, vol. 16, no. 10, (2014).

About the author

Alexis Fernandez-Preiksa is the creator and host of hit podcast *Do You F*cking Mind?* and helps people to align their physical and mindset training every day through no-nonsense, science-backed advice. She's released over 300 episodes of the show since its launch in 2020. She is also the author of *Be Bold: Manifest Your Dream Life* and *The Neuroscience of Self-Love.* She lives in Sydney.